From the Easy Chair – Volume II

GEORGE WILLIAM CURTIS

New York 1894

TABLE OF CONTENTS

GEORGE WILLIAM CURTIS

THE NEW YEAR

N Germany on Sylvesterabend—the eve of Saint Sylvester, the last night of
the year—you shall wake and hear a chorus of voices singing hymns, like
the English waits at Christmas or the Italian pifferari. In the deep silence,
and to one awakening, the music has a penetrating and indefinable pathos,
the pathos that Richter remarked in all music, and which our own Parsons
has hinted delicately—
"Strange was the music that over me stole,
For 'twas born of old sadness that lives in my soul."
There is something of the same feeling in the melody of college songs heard
at a little distance on awakening in the night before Commencement. The
songs are familiar, but they have an appealing melancholy unknown before.
Their dying cadences murmur like a muffled peal heralding the visionary
procession that is passing out of the enchanted realm of youth forever. So
the voices of Sylvester's Eve chant the requiem of the year that is dead. So
much more of life, of opportunity, of achievement, passed; so much nearer
age, decline, the mystery of the end. The music swells in rich and lingering
strains. It is a moment of exaltation, of purification. The chords are dying;
the hymn is ending; it ends. The voices are stilled. It is the benediction of
Saint Sylvester:
"She died and left to me ...
The memory of what has been,
And nevermore will be."
But this is the midnight refrain—The King is dead! With the earliest ray of
daylight the exulting strain begins—Live the King! The bells are ringing; the
children are shouting; there are gifts and greetings, good wishes and

gladness. "Happy New Year! happy New Year!" It is the day of hope and a fresh beginning. Old debts shall be forgiven; old feuds forgotten; old friendships revived. To-day shall be better than yesterday. The good vows shall be kept. A blessing shall be wrung from the fleet angel Opportunity. There shall be more patience, more courage, more faith; the dream shall become life; to-day shall wear the glamour of to-morrow. Ring out the old, ring in the new!

Charles Lamb says that no one ever regarded the first of January with indifference; no one, that is to say, of the new style. But a fellow-pilgrim of the old style, before Pope Gregory retrenched those ten days in October, three hundred years ago, or the British Parliament those eleven days in September, a hundred and thirty-five years ago, took no thought of the first of January. It was a date of no significance. To have mused and moralized upon that day more than upon any other would have exposed him to the mischance against which Rufus Choate asked his daughter to defend him at the opera: "Tell me, my dear, when to applaud, lest unwittingly I dilate with the wrong emotion." The Pope and the Parliament played havoc with the date of the proper annual emotion. Moreover, if a man should happen to think of it, every day is a new-year's day. If we propose a prospect or a retrospect we can stand tiptoe on the top of every day, yes, and of every hour, in the year. Good-morning is but a daily greeting of Happy New Year.

But these smooth generalizations and truisms do not disturb the charm of regularly recurring times and seasons. That the fifth of October, or any day in any month, actually begins a new year, does not give to that date the significance and the feeling of the first of January. Our fellow-pilgrim of the old style must look out for himself. He may have begun his year in March, and a blustering birth it was. But we are children of the new style, and the first of January is our New Year. That is our day of remembrance, our feast of hope, the first page of our fresh calendar of good resolutions, the day of underscoring and emphasis of the swift lapse of life. "A few more of them, and then—" whispers the mentor, who is not deceived by the jolly compliments of the season, and the sober significance of the whisper is plain enough. "Eheu! Posthume," sang the old Roman. "This world and the next, and all's over!" said airy Tom Lackwit to the afflicted widow.

The relentless punctuality, the unwearied urgency, of old Time, who turns his hour-glass with such a sonorous ring on New-Year's Day, seems sometimes a little wanting in the best breeding. It furnishes so unnecessary a register. The slow whitening and thinning of the hair; the gradual incision of wrinkles; the queer antics of the sight, which holds the newspaper at farther and farther removes, until at last it is forced to succumb to glasses; the abated pace in walking; the dexterous avoidance of stone walls in country rambles; the harmless frauds lurking in the expressed reasons for frequent pauses in climbing a hill to turn and see the landscape—frauds which the tears of my Uncle Toby's good angel promptly wash away; the general and gradual adjustment to greater repose—all these surely are adequate reminders and signs of the sovereignty of Time. Why should he be greedy of more? Why thump and rattle at the door, as it were, on the first of January, and bawl out to the whole world that we are a year older, and that makes—!

It is disagreeably unnecessary. Why should not the old fellow do his duty quietly, and tell off another year without such an outrageous uproar? Does he think it so pleasant to hear his increasing tally—forty, five, fifty, five, sixty, five? Peace! peace! Why not have it understood that the tally beyond—well, say fifty, is a gross impertinence? Let something be left to the imagination. Besides, what is the use of wigs and hair-dye and padding, and what not coloring and enamelling, and other juvenescent procedures of the feminine arcana, if annual proclamation of impertinent dates and facts is to be made?

The worst of it is that it is a positive interference with the just play of the fundamental truth that age is not justly measurable by the mere lapse of time. Some people are never young, others defy age. This, indeed, is due to temperament. But that is not all. Those gray hairs and wrinkles, that eyesight of less keenness, that disinclination to leap walls, and those fraudulent halts to survey the rearward landscape, are enemies whose assaults are by no means regular. They come at very different times to different people. Adolphus at sixty despises spectacles. Triptolemus at thirty is bald. The hair of Horatius at sixty-five is as affluent as Hyperion's, and as dark without unguents as the raven's plume. Let facts speak to a candid world. Why should that graybeard Paul Pry called Time blare through a speaking-trumpet that the brave Valentine—

"As wild his thoughts and gay of wing
As Eden's garden bird"—

is just as old as old, toothless, tottering, decrepit Orson?

Every well-regulated citizen of the world is interested, and more vitally interested with every closing year, that upon the point of age all men shall be left to their merits, and shall not be measured arbitrarily by that Procrustean standard of years. It is notorious that men grow wiser every year, and it is observable that the more years they have, the more they look with doubt and questioning upon the Family Record. Those leaves of births following the doubtful books of Scripture, registered with such painful and needless particularity of dates, partake of the doubtfulness of their neighborhood. They are mere intercalations, new books of the Apocrypha. Yet they often cause young fellows of seventy to be accused and convicted of being old men.

Since, then, we cannot stop the flight of Time, let him pass. But he must not calumniate as he passes. He must not be allowed to stigmatize vigor and health and freshness of feeling and the young heart and the agile foot as old merely because of a certain number of years. This is the season of good resolutions. The new year begins in a snow-storm of white vows. So be it. But let our whitest vow be, after that for a whiter life, that age shall no longer be measured by this arbitrary standard of years, and that those deceitful and practical octogenarians of thirty shall not escape as young merely because they have not yet shown the strength to carry threescore and ten with jocund elasticity.

Then Happy New Year shall not mean Good-night, but Good-morrow.

THE PUBLIC SCOLD

THE Easy Chair was lately asked whether it thought the office of public scold an agreeable one. There was a certain tartness in the question, as if its real purpose was to learn from the Easy Chair whether It enjoyed that position, and upon looking further it appeared that the question had been suggested by a remark of the Easy Chair's to the effect that a certain class of our fellow-creatures seemed to be disposed to do their duty in a manner that might be improved. But what is an Easy Chair but a kind of censor morum! Would the kind critic of its conduct have it say to the gentleman whose hands are soiled that they are as pure as the morning, and to the tactless dame who makes all her neighbors uncomfortable that her manners are charming?

Probably this is really what the critic meant, for he continued by saying that it is so much better to dilate upon what is pleasant than to discuss the unpleasant aspects of life. That is true. It was the principle of the Vicar of Bray. That reverend gentleman always avoided friction. He was a chip of the Polonius block. The cloud was a camel or a whale, according to the fancy of his companion. The good vicar looked askance at Rome under Henry and Edward, and told his beads piously under Mary, and upon reflection eschewed the mass-house under Elizabeth. He dilated upon the pleasant aspects of affairs. We can imagine him saying to Ridley in the time of Mary, "My dear bishop, why think yourself wiser than your time?" and a little later to Parker, Elizabeth's Archbishop (Ridley having been burned in the meanwhile), "My dear archbishop, Rome, I see, is much too stringent." The Vicar of Bray was not a scold. He was, according to the abused text, all things to all men.

Yet his profession, our censor must remember, was a scolding profession— at least in the sense in which the word is often used. His duty was to admonish and exhort, to adjure his flock to quit the error of their ways.

Perhaps he was a poor illustration of it. Perhaps, true to his temperament rather than to his profession, instead of urging repentance because the kingdom was at hand, he was accustomed to say: "Brethren, I observe that you lie and steal and slander your neighbors a good deal. But in such a world as this what is to be expected? We are all poor, weak, fallible things. Which of us can hope to strike twelve every time? Let him that thinketh he standeth take heed lest he fall. We must all beware of hypocrisy, dear brethren, and of pretending to be better than our neighbors. You remember the Pharisee who thanked God that he was not as other men. Let him be a warning against the sin of presumption. There is the beautiful lesson of the beam and the mote. We must not forget it. We are all miserable sinners, and therefore we must not twit each other with sinning. We ought to tell the truth, my friends. But we don't. We all lie. Let us therefore not scold each other, since we are all equally wicked. But let us avoid Phariseeism and all that assumption of superior virtue which is implied in saying to a foul-mouthed brother that he ought to speak cleanly. Beware of Phariseeism as of the unpardonable sin. Scold not, dear brethren, but talk of the things which are pleasant, and instead of rebuking the liar, commend his goodness to the poor, and instead of silencing the backbiter, praise his subscription to the soup kitchen. For what says Dr. Watts?

"'Let dogs delight to bark and bite.'

Dogs naturally scold, but we, brethren, we have the gift of avoidance, and, O liars, thieves, and slanderers, let us live together in peace, and say nothing about falsehood, stealing, and calumny."

This was probably the tenor of the sermons of the Vicar of Bray, and this was the way that he strove to save souls. But Fénelon and John Knox and Edwards and Whitefield and Wesley and Channing and St. Paul, each in his own way, said, "Thou art the man," and rebuked both the sin and the sinner. Yet all of them were very human and very fallible, and all came very short of the ideal of duty. To point out a defect in a picture, or to exhort the artist to avoid it, is not to declare yourself an incomparable artist. To demand honesty in public affairs is not to proclaim yourself a saint. To say that school-teachers should be thorough and use their common-sense as well as a text-book is not to scold them. Romilly was not a scold because he denounced the unjust criminal laws, nor John Howard because he rebuked the inhumanity of prisons, nor John the Baptist because he exhorted men to repent.

The poets rebuke our lives by the fair ideals that they draw, but they do not scold. If a man preaches a little sermon illustrating the way in which men in a certain profession, let us say, shirk their duty, and somebody cries out, "Don't scold so!" the preacher may safely exclaim, "Fellow-sinner, thou art the man." But the best illustration is closer at hand. If the Easy Chair reproves certain fellow-sinners for remissness in doing their duty, and for that offence is a scold, what is the censor who scolds the Easy Chair for scolding? Let us avoid Phariseeism, brethren, and the assumption of superior virtue.

NATIONAL NOMINATING CONVENTION

IT was a wise newspaper that recently advised every American who could do so to see a national nominating convention. It is a spectacle visible in no other country, and the most exciting political spectacle in this. It is the arena in which the prolonged and passionate strife of countless ambitions, intrigues, interests, and conspiracies is decided; and it is the more exciting because, with every effort to predetermine the result, the result is still at the mercy of chance. The action of the convention is a lottery. Suddenly, at the decisive moment, an unexpected combination, an impulse, a whim, like an overwhelming tidal wave, sweeps away all plans and calculations, and the result is as complete as it is unanticipated.

Even the device of a two-thirds vote to make a nomination valid does not avail to secure the real preference of the party which the convention represents. The two-thirds rule, as it is called, was designed to baffle the fundamental democratic principle, which is the rule of the majority. When that is abandoned, the proportion selected is purely arbitrary. It may as well be nine tenths as two thirds. But even such a dam will not resist the swelling waters of feeling in a convention. The French say that it is the unexpected that happens, but in a national convention it is the unforeseen which is anticipated. The palpitating multitude, which has been stimulating its own excitement, confronts every doubtful moment with an air which says plainly, "Now it's coming."

There is always a preliminary contest of various cities before the national party committee to decide where the convention shall be held. Local orators with honeyed persuasion dazzle the committee with statistics of the superior convenience, accommodation, beauty, healthfulness, resources, facilities, and whatever else their good genius may suggest, of the city for which each one of them contends. The convention is held in the largest hall, or in a building erected for the purpose, like the Wigwam in Chicago in 1860. The convention itself is composed of about nine hundred state delegates, their seats designated by a flag with the name of the state placed by the seat of the chairman of the delegation. The alternates are also seated. Every convention is full of distinguished leaders and members of the party, and as any of them appears, either entering or rising to speak, they are greeted with great applause. If the temporary chairman be an eminent party chief or an eloquent popular orator, his address touches the springs of emotion and arouses hearty enthusiasm. But the friends of the leading candidates deprecate the mention of names until the candidates are presented by the chosen orator. The reason is that the applause of the convention is one of the counters in the game. There are hired claques in the conventions which keep up a humming cry which is a substitute for applause, and which is sometimes continued for a quarter of an hour. The longer the hum, the more popular the candidate.

Forgetfulness or ignorance of the value of applause under such circumstances reveals the comparative popularity of candidates in the eager mass of delegates and spectators. In one convention the permanent president in his address, but without any sinister purpose, or indeed any other purpose than kindling the convention, mentioned successively, and, of course, with impartial compliment, the name of every candidate who was known to be on the list. Involuntarily he thus tested the feeling of the convention. The galleries also swelled the acclaim, but in the galleries the claque is shrewdly distributed, and in critical moments the approval or disapproval of the turbulent galleries undoubtedly impresses the delegates, and recalls the galleries of the French convention a hundred years ago.

There are occasional skirmishes of debate upon motions or resolutions, but the first great interest of the regular proceedings is the report of the platform committee. It is a tradition of conventions that the platform should be accepted as reported, both to gain the prestige of perfect unanimity and to escape "tinkering," which may lead to endless discussion and discordant feeling. But when the motion is made to proceed to the nomination of candidates, the excitement is intense. The orators are usually carefully selected, not alone as eloquent speakers, but as men of weight and influence, and of what at the moment is more indispensable than everything else—tact. The speeches are made with the fundamental understanding that, however glowing and elaborate the praise of the candidate may be, there shall be an explicit assurance that whatever the merits of any candidate, the candidate who shall be nominated by the convention will receive the universal and enthusiastic support of the party.

On one occasion, when this fundamental rule was forgotten by an ardent orator, who, in the warmth of his devotion to his candidate, declared that no other man was so certain to draw out the whole party vote in the state for which he spoke, a hurricane of hisses from the convention and the galleries silenced him, and the friends of his candidate were instantly aware that a fatal injury had befallen him. In another convention the orator who nominated one of the candidates was so exasperated by what he felt to be the treachery to his candidate of a conspicuous friend of another that his denunciation of the traitor was held to be a covert assault upon the traitor's candidate, and again a tempest of universal hissing overwhelmed the luckless orator and his candidate.

The announcement by states of the first formal vote for candidates is made in impressive silence, followed by immense applause. But the second ballot is more significant; and whenever upon any ballot the announcement of a vote is seen by the tally to decide the nomination, the feeling culminates in an indescribable tumult of frenzied acclamation, and the convention generally adjourns to consider the Vice-Presidency. But the interest in its work is at an end, and it is astounding to see the happy-go-lucky Providence which presides over the selection of the officer who has thrice become the President of the United States.

In the history of national conventions there is no more touching incident than that of Mr. Seward awaiting at his home in Auburn the result of the balloting at the convention of 1860, which nominated Mr. Lincoln. By what is called the logic of the situation Mr. Seward's nomination was assured, and no disappointment could have been greater than the selection of another. How bitter it was was not suspected until his life was recently published! But he encountered the shock with his usual equanimity, and before the election he had made the most extraordinary series of speeches for his party which the annals of any campaign record.

The journal's advice was sound. See a national convention if you can.

BRYANT'S COUNTRY

THE traveller in western Massachusetts, reaching some quiet village upon the hills, which seems to him singularly lonely and remote, often finds some little incident in its annals which connects it with the great world. Coming to Goshen, a solitary little town wholly unknown to most of our readers, he is conscious of the height, of the purity of the air, and the peacefulness of the wooded landscape, and far below, towards the east, he sees the undulating line of Holyoke, and on some fortunate day may catch the gleam of the placid Connecticut winding through broad meadows and between Tom and Holyoke to the Sound.

The little town itself is a grassy street, with a meeting-house and a hotel, which has a desolate air of mistaken enterprise declining into disappointment, with long anticipation of a crowd of summer pilgrims, who might well turn their steps hither, but who have never come. Beyond the village street upon the same plateau is the great Goshen reservoir, which lies hushed in grim repose over the town of Williamsburg, a few miles below, the town which was overwhelmed some years ago by the bursting of the Mill River dam. Such events are the tragedies of the hills, which become traditions told in the village store, and investing with dignity, as the years pass, the villagers who recall the direful day.

Among the traditions of Goshen is that of the passage of some of the soldiers of Burgoyne on their march from Saratoga to Cambridge. When the brilliant British general swept down Lake Champlain to the Hudson, capturing Ticonderoga as he came, it was feared in these hills that he would march triumphantly from Albany to Boston. There was a general rally of all able-bodied men to the rescue; and as they marched away from their fields ripe for the harvest the prospect was dismal, until the able-bodied women marched into the fields and gathered and housed the crops. The British invaders reached Goshen, indeed, on their march from Albany to Boston, but only as prisoners of war.

All this peaceful neighborhood was originally granted by the State to the heirs of soldiers in the early New England wars. Goshen and its neighbor Chesterfield, another city set upon a hill six or seven miles to the south, were grants to the descendants of soldiers in the Narragansett expedition of King Philip's war. From Goshen the Chesterfield meeting-house can be seen against the southern horizon, and the road lies through high pastures and lonely farms to the pleasant town. When you climb its hill and look around, you see a cluster of hospitable houses, around which the neatly kept grounds give an air of refinement to the whole village, which is steeped in rural tranquillity.

The broad hills slope westward towards the valley of the Westfield, and beyond lie the shaggy sides of the Cummington range. Chesterfield has its special tradition of Lafayette passing the night in its old tavern, on his way from Albany to Boston, in 1824. It is a characteristic representative of the hill towns, so still that the air seems drowsy as in Rip Van Winkle's village. But such tranquil towns, in which a moving figure is half spectral and almost a surprise, were the beginnings of the nation. From these sequestered springs the mighty river flows.

Chesterfield has not half the population that it counted seventy years ago. The whole town now reports scarcely seven hundred persons. Yet, with all the old spirit, it invited its neighbors in Hampshire County to come and dine on one of the loveliest of summer days this year. It was the annual festival of the Hill-side Agricultural Society, and fully a thousand people filled the friendly town. The feast was spread upon tables on a green space beside the old house in which Lafayette slept, and under a bower of leafy white birch boughs. The magnates of the county were all present, and it was whispered privately that there were private whisperings among eminent politicians, who, however, with the non-political, or the political of the wrong side, talked cheerfully of the charming day and the promising crops. Politics is the breath of our patriotic nostrils, and it was a stimulating thought that while we were listening to the humorous but well-merited praises of Strawberry Hill pork, some of our bland companions were saving their bacon in other ways; and while we dreamed of crisp sausages and savory ham, were contriving Senators and Councillors, and even a Governor himself.

The simple courtesy and universal intelligence were of the old New England, nor less so the composure and ease with which speaker after speaker mounted the bench on which he sat, and in what he said, and the way in which he said it, showed that he was a graduate of the town meeting. The pastor of Goshen, asked to speak of some of the more noted citizens of the neighboring towns, might well have occupied with so fruitful a text all the hours until sunset. But with exemplary discretion he mentioned but a few, and among them some that surprised a New-Yorker, who had not known, but might have guessed, that Gideon Lee, former Mayor of the city, and Luther Bradish, Lieutenant-Governor of the State, came from the little town upon the Cummington hills opposite, where Bryant studied law.

The whole region before us, indeed, was especially Bryant's. Upon the slope yonder he was born, and we could see the house in which as a boy he lived. "Thanatopsis" was the hymn of his meditations among those solitary woods. There, upon the nearer hill, high over Plainfield, where he wrote the poem the "Water-fowl," forever floating in the twilight heavens—

"Far through their rosy depths dost thou pursue
Thy solitary way."

We were looking upon the cradle of American literature. Here its first enduring poem was written. The poet himself never escaped the spell of the hills. The child was father of the man. Bryant in the city was always the grave and unchanged genius of New England. The city did not wear off the rusticity of his manner. His air was reserved and remote, and he was still wrapped in the seclusion of the hills. It is in such scenes and among such people on such a day that the power of these hills and their influence upon our national life and literature are perceived.

These hidden springs have overflowed the prairies of the West; and how much of the wealth and prosperity, the energy, industry, and enlightenment of New York have trickled down from them, you may hear, if you doubt, every year on Forefathers' Day at the New England dinner in New Amsterdam. As there is altogether too much glory to be adequately celebrated in one day, another has been added, to accommodate the Yankee city of Brooklyn, and it is not the fault of the sons of New England if on those two days the whole continent does not hear the melodious thunder of their eloquence proclaiming that New England always led, is leading still, and will lead forever, the triumphal procession of American progress.

Supported by such a history it is a natural boast. There is, however, one inexorable condition. To do what New England has done, New England must be what she has been.

THE GAME OF NEWPORT

THERE is nothing more delightful than the gravity with which the game of Newport is played. To assist at one of the solemn "functions" like a coach parade is not unlike attendance upon a function of the ancient Church in Rome. On a true Newport afternoon, as soft and sweet and luminous an air as can be breathed, Newport, in every kind of stately and comfortable and light and graceful carriage, with the finest horses and the most loftily disdainful of coachmen, proceeds down the avenue to behold the stately procession along the ocean drive.

Of its kind there is no more beautiful drive in the world. The shore winds among rocks which are massed, a shrewd-eyed traveller said, as on the shores of Greece. The bold character of the coast of Rhode Island and its picturesque effects are wholly unknown upon its neighbor Long Island. The endless reach of sand and the monotony of the vast level land on Long Island have a certain vague charm as of a sea-shore becoming or about to become picturesque. But that point is fully reached by its northern neighbors of the New England coast, and the ocean drive in Newport is in itself incomparable.

For its company on the day of a great social function it is quite as incomparable. Hyde Park, the Bois, the Cascine, the Prater, show no such sumptuous display. If the street boy were a philosopher, he would say, probably, as he watched the spectacle, "My eyes! money plays here for all it is worth." The American street boy of every degree is not supposed to need any stronger impression of the value of money than he already possesses. But Newport is the great school for that instruction, and it is open free to the whole world. Money elsewhere has the same instincts and desires. But in a city, in winter, its sports and effects, however splendid, are divided and hidden. In summer Newport they are concentrated under most fortunate conditions and proceed in the open air.

It is all the more striking because money has built its summer city close by and just above one of the oldest and most historic of our cities. It has improvised its magnificence and mad profusion upon the outskirts of simplicity and moderation are observant, for all their plainness. When they were asked what effect the new town produced upon the old, whether the rollicking city on the hill harmed or helped the plodding seaport, they answered: "Until Crœsus and Midas came, it was beneficial. But they have ruined Newport."

Perhaps not, however. The Newport on the hill of to-day is the legitimate offspring of the earlier summer retreat. That was a group of the select who came to Newport to enjoy themselves for the summer. They were well-to-do, some of them. But not many dwelt in cottages. The multitude lived in hotels. They danced, they dined, they drove, they sauntered. It was the green tree. It was less money enjoying itself as more money enjoys itself now. The gossip, the flirting, the display were not of another kind, they were the same as to-day, but the scale was more limited. Mrs. Candour, Mrs. Malaprop, Sir Benjamin Backbite, and the brothers Surface were already there. The standards of conduct, the ideals of honor, were not essentially different.

A generation ago Sir Benjamin bowed and danced and supped at Mrs. Malaprop's ball with all the gay world of that time, which is now in wigs, caps, turbans, or heaven; and the next day, dining with Mrs. Candour, Sir Benjamin told, with infinite relish and to the great amusement of the table, the story of his hostess's verbal trips and stumbles. It did not seem to be conduct essentially base, because this sparkling summer realm by the sea is like Charles Lamb's conception of the artificial comedy of the eighteenth century: "I confess, for myself, that, with no great delinquencies to answer for, I am glad for a season to take an airing beyond the diocese of the strict conscience—not to live always in the precincts of the law courts—but now and then, for a dream-while or so, to imagine a world with no meddling restrictions, to get into recesses whither the hunter cannot follow me—

"'secret shades

Of wooded Ida's inmost grove

While yet there was no fear of Jove.'"

To take permanent lodgings beyond the diocese of the strict conscience, however, is a critical enterprise. If you take a house in Capua, you must needs breathe the Capuan air. The magnetic rock in Sindbad's story drew out the nails of the ships that ventured too near. Old Mithridates fed on poisons until they "became a kind of nutriment," as Dr. Rappaccini fed his daughter, until, too late, he discovered that she was doomed. The graybeards who drive out to see the coach parade, and recall the days, before the ocean drive, when the rocks beyond Lily Pond were a glimmering land of Beulah, may prattle of the golden age of Newport as of a happy past in which the graybeards were born. But will they seriously contend that the age of Crœsus and Midas is not the golden age of Newport?

While they are gossiping, the coaches approach. They have been through the town, and are driving out by the Fort road; and as they appear, the vast throng of carriages which have driven out to meet them pull to the side of the road to allow a free course. A multitude of spectators awaiting a festal procession, which at last is coming, naturally suggests applause. But there is profound silence. There is no cheer for every spectator to catch up and pass on. The first coach is at hand, and gravely passes at a deliberate pace, and the great world in carriages gravely looks on. The second coach deliberately follows, and is surveyed with equal gravity. The next perhaps will strike a spark of applause. But the next passes deliberately amid a silence profound. One friend, perhaps, in the stately procession gravely nods to another gravely gazing from a carriage. The "function" proceeds. Far out at sea the white sails flash, and the summer surf breaks gently along the shore. Every coach rolls slowly by. The moment for cheering has not yet arrived. Indeed, it does not arrive before the pageant has passed, and the reviewing carriages are turning and following on in its wake. It is truly a solemn function. Graybeard recalls nothing like it for multitude and display in the old drives on "beach days" along the beach in what he calls the golden age. But does he doubt that old Newport would have done it gladly if it could have done it?

If the ghost of Heliogabalus haunts the villa'd shore, it is with no hope of resuming the imperial crown. His court merely makes a pretty summer spectacle when the opera ends. The coach and the stately equipage and the flashing splendor of busy idleness are the pageant which is kindly displayed gratis for the passengers in the omnibus, for the pedestrians and the nurses. They sit and stroll and stare at their ease while the gay play proceeds before their eyes. Nowhere more constantly than in the summer Newport does the remark of the little child watching the march of the soldiers recur—"Mamma, how good they are to make such a show!"

THE LECTURE LYCEUM

THE Utica Herald in a pleasant article recently recalled the lecture lyceum of a quarter of a century ago. It was then what is called a power. It greatly influenced public opinion. Its spirit was indicated by the reply of Wendell Phillips to an invitation which asked him his terms and his subject. He answered that for a literary lecture he should expect a hundred dollars, but he would deliver an antislavery address for nothing, and pay his own expenses. The lecturers who were most sought at that time were almost without exception men of very strong convictions upon the great question which, however evaded and dexterously hidden, was the vital thought of the country; and every successive week from November to April, in the largest cities and the smallest cities, along the belt of country from the Kennebec through New England and New York westward through Ohio and the Northwest to the Mississippi, before thousands of the most intelligent American citizens, this band of lecturers advanced, like a well-ordered platoon of sharp-shooters, and delivered their destructive volley at what they felt to be the common enemy.

Edward Everett, "the monarch of the platform," as Mr. Edward Parker called him in his book upon American contemporary orators, during part of this same time was making a tour through much of the same region with his oration upon Washington, for the benefit of the fund for the purchase of Mount Vernon, and he was also writing the Mount Vernon papers for the Ledger, in one of which he gave an entertaining description of a night in a sleeping-car, when those itinerant bedchambers had but recently taken to the road. Mr. Everett's conservative temperament made his oration a kind of corrective of the influence of the great tendency of the lyceum lecture. But patriotic as his purpose undoubtedly was, his effort to stem the rapidly rising tide of public sentiment was like the protests of Governor

Hutchinson and the Colonial conservatives against the fervid revolutionary appeals of Otis and Adams and Quincy. Other popular speakers of the same sympathy as that of Mr. Everett found themselves out of tune with the lyceum audience, and were but meteors flashing across the stage, whose light was lost in the steady and increasing glow of the group of men who were identified with the great day of the lyceum lecture. These men were not all like Wendell Phillips, open leaders of a specific agitation, nor were these lectures always ostensibly upon what are called public questions. But the influence of the lecturers was unmistakable. They were all men known to be in the strongest sympathy with the most advanced feeling of the agitation. It was the plain spirit and tone and drift of those lectures, an occasional allusion and the necessary application of the remarks, however general, to the actual situation, rather than any deliberate discussion of the question itself, which characterized the lyceum of that day. There was sometimes an attempted reaction against this tendency. In Philadelphia it was discovered that colored persons were not admitted to the Musical Fund Hall, in which the lectures had been given. The leading lecturers instantly informed the committee that they declined to speak in the hall so long as the restriction continued. In Albany the reactionary sentiment in the Young Men's Association succeeded in electing a lecture committee which was resolved upon a purely "literary" course, and which would not invite the usual lecturers. The result was an independent course, under the auspices of dissatisfied members of the association, in which the rejected lecturers spoke in the largest hall in the city, and the signal triumph of the seceders lay in the immense audience which assembled in contrast to the attenuated attendance upon the regular course.

The singular success of the lyceum lecture of that time was due, undoubtedly, to two causes—the simultaneous appearance of a remarkable group of orators, and their profound sympathy with the question which absorbed the public mind. The weekly lecture was not merely a display of oratory, not only an amusing recreation, but it brought wit and accomplishment and eloquence to strengthen the public feeling and arouse the public conscience, and to confirm the earnest spirit which was universal, and which forecast the great events and the noble elevation of the public mind that followed. Emerson, Wendell Phillips, Gough, Beecher, Chapin, Starr King, Theodore Parker, could of themselves carry any course of lectures, and each in his own way was thoroughly in accord with the truest American life of that time. The situation and the condition of the public mind would not have availed, indeed, without the happy chance of such orators to create the lyceum, but with that chance the lyceum of that day was as remarkable a continuous display of various and effective eloquence as has been ever known.

If the faithful diary of any lecturer who went the grand rounds twenty-five years ago, from Maine to the Mississippi, could be published, it would be full of the most amusing stories. The lecturers all had them to tell, and they were all men of a singularly fine perception of humor. James T. Fields, the publisher in Boston, was the friend of all the lyceum orators, and towards the close of his life he was himself a popular and attractive lecturer upon literary subjects. His little cell or private office in the old corner book-store in Boston was an exchange of lecturers for that neighborhood, which teemed with lyceums, and no similar space has ever heard fresher stories better told, or has ever echoed with gayer laughter.

It was the pleasant company in that little retreat which first heard, the day after it occurred, the tale of the belated lecturer who, hurrying from the cars in a carriage to the hall in Boston, long beyond the hour, dinnerless, and with no chance to dress, opened his travelling-bag, and proceeded, to the consternation of the lady who had taken a seat in the same carriage, and whose pardon he politely and briefly invoked, to change his collar and his coat. As he began to pull off his coat, having pulled off his collar, his amazed and terrified fellow-passenger began to pull at the door, and to call loudly upon the driver, who was furiously whipping his horses into a pace that increased both the noise of the carriage and the conviction of the terrified lady that she was the victim of some dreadful conspiracy, or the hapless victim of a maniac. The maniac's earnest but interjectional explanation as he proceeded in his toilet, begging his companion to be pacified, as he was merely going to lecture, was an unintelligible asseveration, which only made his madness more indisputable and awful, and what might have befallen the poor lady, if the carriage had not suddenly stopped at the hall, and the lecturer, in his clean collar and black coat, had not begged her pardon for frightening her, with a fervor that frightened her all the more, and disappeared from the vehicle with his travelling-bag, shawl, and umbrella, he was not prepared to say. But the tale, as he told it the next morning with infinite humor in Fields's corner, was received, as he ruefully admitted, with louder shouts of laughter than had greeted the brightest witticisms of his lecture.

Fields is gone, and his old friend and neighbor Whipple, who was one of the earliest of the noted lyceum lecturers. The old corner in the old corner book-store is gone, and with it have vanished many of the happy company that gathered there, not only of orators, but of famous authors. The lyceum of the last generation is gone, but it is not surprising that those who recall with the Utica Herald its golden prime should cherish a kindly and regretful feeling for an institution which was so peculiarly American, and which served so well the true American spirit and American life.

TWEED

THERE are many persons who wonder why Tweed did not evade justice by forfeiting his bail. He had every chance to escape, they say; why did he stay? His chief confederates are safe in Europe, where he might easily have been, yet he was foolish enough to take the risk of a trial, and he is imprisoned, probably for the rest of his life. The explanation, however, is very obvious. He did not believe there was any risk. Tweed was the most striking illustration of a very common faith—belief in the Almighty Dollar. He is the victim of a most touching fidelity to the great principle which every good American will surely be the last to flout. His creed was very simple: it was that money would buy everything, and he reposed upon his belief with the sweet security of the Mussulman who sees by faith a heaven of houris. Certainly his confidence was not surprising. He had proved his creed. He had seen money work miracles. He had seen himself, a man of no cleverness and of no advantages, rising swiftly by means of it from insignificant poverty to the control of a great party. It had made him master of one of the great cities of the world. It had secured for him Governors, Legislatures, councils, and legal and executive authorities of every kind. He invested in land and judges. He bought dogs and lawyers. He silenced the press with a golden muzzle, and money made his will law.

Here was a man who wanted nothing that money could not buy: was it strange that he had unbounded faith in it? Every form of virtue was to him mere affectation, a more or less ingenious and tenacious "strike" for money. If a man spoke of honesty, patriotism, self-respect, the public welfare, public opinion, truth, justice, right, Tweed smiled at the fine phrases in which the auctioneer, anxious to sell himself, cried, "Going! going!" Argument, reason, decency—they were meaningless to him. If an opponent held out, he simply asked, "How much?" The world was a market. Life was

29

a bargain. He felt himself with pride to be the largest operator in his way, as Vanderbilt in his, or Stewart in his.

In Albany he had the finest quarters at the Delavan, and when he came into the great dining-room at dinner-time, and looked at all the tables thronged with members of the Legislature and the lobby, he had a benignant, paternal expression, as of a patriarch pleased to see his retainers happy. It was a magnificent rendering of Fagin and his pupils. You could imagine him trotting up and down in the character of an unsuspicious old gentleman with his handkerchief hanging out of his pocket, that his scholars might show their skill in prigging a wipe. He knew which of that cheerful company was the Artful Dodger and which Charley Bates. And he never doubted that he could buy every man in the room if he were willing to pay the price. So at the Capitol, where sits the Legislature of a noble commonwealth of four millions of souls, he moved about with an air of fat good-nature, like the chief shepherd of the flock. If he stood at the door of the Assembly looking in, it is easy to fancy him saying to himself, The State pays these men two or three hundred dollars for four months' service; I will give them better wages. He did not doubt that it was a fair transaction. What is the State? It is only four millions of people, he thought, who are all trying to be rich—struggling, cheating, by hook or by crook, every man for himself, and the devil take the hindmost, to be rich. These men would be fools not to take my money. And he smiled his fat smile, and paid liberally for all that was in market.

There were some papers, whose price he could not ascertain, which persisted in speaking ill of him and his pals. If the fools did not know their own interest enough to be content with a good price—say, of corporation advertising—they must be silenced. The conceit of virtue must not be pushed too far. So one day his Legislature passed a bill virtually giving his judges power to imprison editors at their pleasure. But virtue—that is, in the Tweed theory of life, obstinacy in holding out for a higher price—mustered such a really respectable protest that the public project of coercion failed, and private methods were tried. Tweed had no doubt that reputation could be bought as well as power. Peter Cooper builds an institute for the education of the poor, does he? You mean, said Tweed, a monument to his own glory. He pays a certain number of thousands of dollars for the reputation of philanthropy. And Mr. Stewart builds a working-woman's palace. Ah! And Mr. Astor founds a library. Indeed! And they are benevolent gentlemen and benefactors of their kind? Not at all. They merely invest money in a certain kind of fame. That pleases their taste, as fast horses and yachts and pictures please the taste of other people. I will show you how 'tis done, says the faithful believer in the Dollar. And he gives fifty thousand dollars to the poor just as winter is beginning. "Let the cavillers say what they will," exclaim a myriad voices, "that shows a good heart." Tweed, as it were, tips a wink. I told you how it was done, he seems to say: what is there that money will not buy?

Is it surprising that such a man did not try to evade justice? Justice in his view was a commodity like legislative honor, like newspaper independence, like the reputation of benevolence. The reform movement was to him a sudden and confusing flurry, in which strikers, to whose terms he would not yield, had somehow gained a momentary advantage. He had perhaps made a mistake in not buying them at their own price. Success had possibly put him off his guard. He was sure that if an indictment were found, that would be the end of it, and he had no feeling of shame. His friend Fisk had shown what lawyers were made of, and he himself would buy lawyers and judges, sheriffs and juries. He knew that the one thing that in a needy and greedy world cannot fail is money. He came to his first trial, and the jury disagreed: naturally, for he had bought some of them. The evidence is, of course, moral only, but it is conclusive. If justice, facetiously so called, wanted another bout, he would "come up smiling." There was no trick or quibble that lawyers could devise for which he had not made munificent preparation, even to asserting that the judge who obstinately refused to name a price was disqualified from sitting at the trial. Money had never failed before; it certainly would not at this last pinch.

But it did, and the bewilderment and consternation of this simple devotee were pitiful. He had but one article in his faith, and that was now destroyed. He had staked everything upon the certainty of the Almighty Dollar, and he had lost. But there was something not less noticeable than his unquestioning faith. It was that his faith was so generally held. For what gave the universal and intense interest to the Tweed trial? Here was a common thief, except in the amount of his theft, of whose guilt nobody had any doubt, against whom, as the judge said, the evidence was a mathematical demonstration, and his conviction was hailed as a kind of national deliverance and vindication of human justice. There was but one reason for this, and it was the feeling that money would free him. Of course it was known that the judge could not be bought, nor the Attorney-General, nor the prosecution. Tweed might as well have offered to buy the moral law. But public knowledge ended there. And in the degree of the universality of the belief that somehow, by actual bribery, or by legal quirk or shift or sham, money would buy him off, is the value of the lesson of his conviction, which is that the utmost power of money fails before firm, sagacious, and intelligent honesty. There is not a saloon in New York in which the Tweed contempt of honorable motives is the sole faith which has not had an astounding revelation, and learned that money is not omnipotent.

Those saloons have learned one other thing—that stealing is the same crime, whether it be the theft of public or of private property. The Robin

Hood jollity that surrounded Tweed, his familiar name, the "Boss," the laughing stories that were told of him, showed that he was held in very different estimation from an ordinary thief. The baser newspapers evidently regarded him as the French nobleman regarded himself who was firmly convinced that the Almighty would think twice before condemning such a gentleman as he. So when Tweed went to the Tombs the same feeling attended him. The officers could not believe that it was really meant so rich a man, who had lived in so fine a house, and had spent money so profusely, should be treated as a common offender. The wretch who steals a loaf to feed his starving children must have short shrift, and Black Maria despatches him at the earliest moment. But a "statesman" who steals millions of dollars from the people—really the law must think twice before handling him impolitely! A day or two after he had been taken to jail, on his way to the penitentiary, the papers said, as if he had been a beloved prisoner of state whom cruel governments might torture, but whom the people would still honor: "A great many improvements have been made in his cell by his friends, and it has now quite a cosey, comfortable appearance. The floor is covered with a carpet of a dark green ground. The walls are hung with dark green cloth, and the panes in the windows, opening on Centre Street, which were cracked and broken a few days ago, have been newly glazed. In the centre of the room is a large round table, at which the 'Boss' takes his three regular meals, served up in the best manner from the prison restaurant. There is a luxurious leather-covered lounge in one corner, and five chairs, including a large, comfortable rocking-chair. Besides these few articles of furniture are a wash-stand and a book-case. The prisoner is plentifully supplied with reading matter; and as for creature comforts, the solicitude of his friends and relatives leaves nothing to be desired except liberty. Crowds of people have called to see him for the past two days, but none were admitted without passes from the Commissioners."

This feeling was akin to that which inspires the proverb and the practice that "all's fair at the Custom-house." When Robin Hood stepped politely to the door of my Lord Bishop's carriage and requested him to alight under the greenwood tree, and proceeded to rifle the carriage of all the treasure that his lordship was conveying, he was not felt to be a common thief. Far from it; he was the people's tax-gatherer in green. He scattered with a free hand among the poor the money which the rich man could lose without feeling it. Nobody suffered. My Lord Bishop was admonished that he had the poor always with him, and the poor rejoiced in his involuntary largess. So "the boys" thought of Tweed. While the "Boss" was king there was always money about, as they said; and when did Robin Hood himself ever bestow fifty thousand dollars in a lump upon the poor? Besides, who could say that he was robbed? The rich could not feel it; and was any poor orphan defrauded by him, any poor widow pinched, any honest laborer burdened?

Yes, they were. It was public money that he stole. And what is public money? It is the taxes. And who pay the taxes—the rich? No, the poor, the producers. They come out of the rent of the tenement-house; out of the price of tea and sugar and coal; out of the pittance of the widow and orphan, and the small wages of the laborer. It was from the poor who cowered gratefully over the coal that he gave them that he stole the coal. His confederate, Sweeny, planted hyacinths in the city parks, and for every flower some poor soul was pinched. Gay Robin Hood strips the baron, and the poor bless him as he flings them the gold. Then the baron goes home to his castle and wrings teeth out of the jaws of Isaac of York, to force him to give money. Then Isaac of York advances at a more ruinous rate than yesterday the interest upon the money he lends. So when Tweed steals from the public treasury he picks every private pocket. Every stroke of his hammer, if he hammers stone with other thieves, refreshes in the public mind these familiar truths. It is humiliating that the conviction of an evident offender in a court of law should be a cause of public congratulation. But, on the other hand, it is cheering that shameless crime intrenched in every way, and defying the course of law, should by that course be quietly convicted and surely punished.

COMMENCEMENT

IT is a changed college world since Nat. Willis's Philip Slingsby was the hero of many a maiden's dream, and the stories of Willis reflected the modest gayety of the society of his time. Nahant was then a summer resort of importance, and had not become, as one of its denizens said in later years, only "cold Boston." Willis's heroes, like Byron's, were largely himself, and it was but a thin veil that covered in them persons familiar in the society that he knew, and incidents drawn from his own experience.

He was the college hero of his time. But his Scripture poems, which had great vogue and were printed in all the "classbooks" and "readers," and his "Burial of Arnold," a young and brilliant Senior at Yale, and his bright and blithe "Saturday Afternoon," are quite passed out of current knowledge. They are not the kind of verse which is produced in college now. Their Byronic sentimentality is not to the taste of the college club and Greek Letter Society man of to-day; and Charles Coldstream, who looks on listlessly at the college athletic games, leaves enthusiasm to "the Fresh," and has "really never read those things of Willis's."

Yet the dominant emotions of Commencement this year were very much what they were when Philip Slingsby dared the waltz, and even the more emancipated belles shuddered a little as they slid into the charmed circle. Youth and hope and the passion which "is not all a dream" are forever renewed, and if the fashion changes, the substance remains. In the crowded church at Commencement this year, with the gay dresses and the flowers and the music and the soft summer air breathing in at the open doors and windows, there are still palpitating bosoms, and a color that comes and goes, and glances that meet and mingle—"read the language of those wandering eye-beams—the heart knoweth."

It was "Nat. Willis" yesterday, in a high-collared coat and an ample cravat such as Brummel wore, and even D'Orsay. It is a quaint and a droll costume, as you see it in those old Fraser pictures of English authors "'tis sixty years since." But in that guise it is you, sir, of to-day, and if your oration is spoken to one auditor, in all that lovely throng in the gallery, whose heart answers "pity Zekle" to your pitapat, do you think that the divine Una's grandmother was never young, and that the droll high-collared coats did not cover hearts as sensitive and hopes as high as the faultless summer attire of Nameless, Jun., class of '90? The actors change, but the spectacle is the same. Even the members of the reverend and venerable the corporation, those bald and white-haired worthies who seem vaguely always to have been sitting unchanged in the front pews, like those austere senators of Rome of whom the tradition tells us that they sat motionless although the invader came—even they are living monuments, and on their hearts, as on tablets, the story of the wandering eye-beams is engraved.

There is not one of the young heroes of the Commencement hour whom those elders do not scan with knowledge. These wise young judges carry no secrets which the elders do not share. Is it a strange world that of Willis and his Philip Slingsby? It is the world of the moment and of this Commencement.

But there is something else in Commencement besides this romance of feeling and tradition. It is the celebration of the intellectual life. The eloquence, indeed, is sometimes rather copious. An oration in the morning before one literary society; in the afternoon before another; and a sermon in the evening before the Missionary Association, is good measure heaped up and running over. There is some jealousy also even in academic groves. In the older day, if the Melpomene had its oration in the morning and the Euterpe in the afternoon, and you read on the following Sunday, scrawled on the blank page of the hymn-book in the pew, "Words, words, words, oration of Cicero," and "Genius, eloquence, common-sense, oration of Demosthenes," you knew that you read the comment upon the rival orator of a Melpomenean or a Euterpean, as the case might be. But if the orator was not always wise or eloquent, there were also discourses which have profoundly influenced the lives of those who heard or read them, giving a direction and inspiring a fidelity which, like Wordsworth's thoughts of his past years, breed perpetual benediction.

It is a recollection blended of many feelings, that which the recurring Commencement brings to the alumnus. But the deep and permanent charm is the consciousness of the infinite worth and consolation of letters. Theoretically the college course was a series of years devoted to making acquaintance with the treasures of human genius. Possibly there was in fact some divergence from the theory. But that was the opportunity. The gates were set ajar, and if the neophyte did not choose to enter, he lost—as the teacher said to his pupil who went fishing rather than to hear Webster's eulogy on Adams and Jefferson—he lost what he can never regain.

Is there some fatality which makes the pen that treats of Commencement hortatory and didactic? Is there some secret charm which still allies the college to the pulpit, so that to talk about it is presently to begin to preach? The Easy Chair asks because it feels that it is about to take the sacerdotal tone, and remind the youth who is leaving or entering college that, like every other epoch in life, college is an opportunity. It is what you make it. Fate, as the older times would have said—life, as we prefer to say—gives us a chance. But the improvement of it we give ourselves. The tragedy of the refrain, "Too late, too late; ye cannot enter now," is that of the man who, in our simple phrase, wasted his college years. The tender spell of Whittier's "Maud Muller" lies in its saddest words of tongue or pen. But the memory of what might have been is so profoundly pathetic because it might not have been, and we were the arbiters of fate and did not choose to turn upward.

Kind sir of the college, who lend to the preacher of the moment your listening ear, the preacher himself may be a wearisome chaplain, but you are the young judge of the summer afternoon, smelling the meadows sweet with hay, and stopping at the cool spring where Maud Muller hands you the refreshing draught. Do you follow the allegory, and see in that maid what really she is? To you she is a maiden who rakes the hay; to Numa she was Egeria by the other fountain. It is a sweet illusion, for the maid is not Egeria nor Maud Muller, but under those gentle forms she is the nymph of opportunity. Woo her and win her, and all the happiness that might have been will be yours.

There is nothing more touching than the inability of the chooser to comprehend the choice. Why did not the judge yield to the soft persuasion of that simple loveliness? Why did he not embrace the opportunity, and fold his happiness to his heart? Well, sir, that is always the question. But if he did not know that in that fair figure opportunity stood before him, you do know it. Don't be satisfied to hum "in court an old love tune." You remember the legend of the Sibyl's books. Was it interpreted to you in the class-room? Do you interpret it to yourself?

The most inspiring tradition in every college is not that of the boat or the ball, of copious gold and flowing wine, of Milo or Sardanapalus or Midas; it is not that of the "dig" or the "prig," of Dryasdust or Casaubon; but it is that of the youth, by whatever name he was called in your college, who did not, like the judge, "closing his heart," ride on—who knew that four such years as yours in college would never return, and that they offered him the golden keys which, polished by his labor, would open the heaped treasures of genius in all ages and lands. It is he who in taking the keys did not grudge the labor, and to whose life those treasures have been wide open.

No, the inspiring personal tradition of college was not the pleasant Philip

Slingsby; it was rather Philip Sidney, who rode with the best and was a man in every manly enterprise, but who had so used his opportunities in study and affairs that Hubert Languet, most accomplished of scholars, called him friend, and William of Orange called him master.

THE STREETS OF NEW YORK

EVEN the Pan-Americans protest that the streets of New York are dirty. It is very comical, but it is true, that all our marvellous prosperity, our genius of invention, our quickness of wit, and profusion of resource; all our patriotism and pride, our great traditions of liberty and heroism, our free soil, free speech, and free press; and all the force and intelligence of our free government—cannot keep the streets of New York clean. Miss Edwards, the most courteous and friendly of visitors, is compelled to say: "I found on all sides nothing but holes of mud, gutters, and dirt piles, an endless rush and a block of street traffic. There are so many dangers and the state of the highways is such as to make it incomprehensible to English people that enterprising Americans would long endure it."

Miss Edwards is familiar with the dirt of Egypt, which is universal and intolerable, but even that does not mollify or alleviate the awful impression of dirty New York. Then a Pan-American, perhaps from Bogota, from Callao, from Lima, from Santiago, from Buenos Ayres, from Rio de Janeiro, from Guayaquil—cities in which we had not supposed impeccable highways to be—politely flagellates us, and ignominiously discrowns Broadway. "It was impossible not to notice the deplorable condition of the streets. Our carriages plunged terribly into the holes which at frequent intervals were met with, and the wheels at every turn sent whirls of mud, which compelled the passers-by to keep at a respectful distance."

We may indeed reply that this is the fling of a Pan-American. And who, forsooth, is a Pan-American? Is he the superior—nay, does he presume to be the peer—of a North American? Are we not notoriously the greatest nation in the world? Does not our population reduplicate incalculably? Have we not carried civilization from sea to sea? Have we not the largest lakes, the longest rivers, the broadest prairies, the greatest cataract, in the world? And shall the minions of monarchies and the pigmies of tuppenny temporary republics snap their ridiculous fingers at us, and presume to say that the streets of New York are dirty? The idea is preposterous. It is contemptible. Moreover, it is insulting, and the streets of New York are—

It is plain sailing—or slipping, as chance may determine whether we go in the water or the mud—so far, but it is a little difficult to end that sentence in the same key. Let us try another, possibly a little less perfervid. The population of the United States is some sixty millions. Taken altogether they form undoubtedly the most intelligent community, with the highest average well-being, in the world. They are self-governing down to aldermen and coroners. More than in any country at any time in history, the will of the majority of the adult male population determines the government. The city of New York is one of the three or four chief cities of the world. It is confessedly the metropolis of this blessed and absolutely self-governing country, and the streets of New York can't be kept clean.

Is there any possible method of describing the unquestionable greatness and undoubted glory of the country, its resplendent history and its miraculous achievements, in an ascending and cumulative series of epithets and epigrams which shall end truthfully in the resounding allegation, "and the streets of New York are kept clean"? Indeed, is not this little joker worse than that of the thimble? Does he not grin at us from every pile of mud, and laugh out of every hole, and snicker and sneer on every side of the unremoved and apparently irremovable dirt and disorder?

It is absurd, as the boys say, to "blame" this situation upon somebody else—some street commissioner, or scavenger, or other officer, or employé. Nobody is ever guilty of misrule in this country but the rulers, and the rulers are the people. The citizens of New York elect the city officers who are to do the city work which the citizens pay for. They give some of those officers authority to dismiss others who are derelict in their duty, and the governor can deal with the chief officers who do not obey the command of the people. If the taxes are outrageously heavy, if the money is squandered, if the streets are dirty and city government a farce, nobody is to blame but the citizens. They have as good a government as they choose, and the kind of government they desire.

Then they desire dirty streets? Certainly. That is to say, they don't desire clean streets strongly enough to secure them. Then popular government has failed in cities? Rather there are some things in cities in which popular government is not especially interested. If there are two hundred and fifty thousand voters in the city of New York, how many of them really care enough for clean streets and proper municipal administration to spend time and trouble to secure them?

Consider the lilies of the field—that is to say, look at the aldermen and the municipal officers, the representatives in the State Legislature and in

40

Congress that the city of New York elects. Do they represent what we call its intelligence and character? Yet undeniably they are representatives of the majority of the voters, and if that majority be corrupt or stupid, it is either because there are more knaves and fools than intelligent and honest citizens among the voters, or because such citizens do not care to take the trouble to vote and to be represented; in which case the Aldermen and Co. that we see are, morally speaking, true representatives of the city. The minions of monarchies and the pigmies of tuppenny temporary republics, as they bump and wallow and flounder, bespattered and contemptuous, through the streets of New York, may truly say that they are such streets as the citizens desire, because if the people desired clean streets, unless popular government be a failure, they would have them. If the mayor did not appoint officers who would clean the streets, they would require the governor to deal with the mayor.

Does it necessarily follow, because popular government is, upon the whole, the best government, that the governing people desire all good things that government can supply? Liberty they want, and equality, and fair play; but do they, because they are self-governing, desire beautiful buildings and clean streets? Might not a good-natured despot of fine taste and sanitary enlightenment and a sense of order give his dominions nobler public works and a better municipal administration than a republic which is neither tuppenny nor temporary, but in which there is easy and indolent indifference to public beauty and public order?

"Above all," said the English bishop to the young catechumen, "don't mistake zeal for knowledge." Above all, says the good genius of America, don't confound national bumptiousness with patriotism.

THE MORALITY OF DANCING

THE gravity of the discussion of the morality of dancing is exceedingly amusing. The dancing of young people is as natural and instinctive as their laughing and singing, and the old Easy Chairs about the wall might as wisely quarrel with the song of the bobolink in the fields as with the dance upon the floor. But the grave censors who condemn it must be heard. There is reason in the way in which they often put their objections. Excitement, late hours, exposure of health, all these are bad. But, on the other hand, exercise, cheerfulness, friendly conversation, all these are good. The zealous censors confound uses and abuses. The Easy Chair has seen a worthy temperance apostle ingulfing cups of coffee in the pauses of an exhortation to abstinence, until it marvelled at the capacity of the apostolic stomach. Could there be no intemperance in coffee-drinking? But was coffee not to be drunk? The Easy Chair has seen such frantic gobbling at a railway eating-room that it could only gaze in wonder at the sottish and, so to speak, drunken eating. But is food not to be eaten? The Easy Chair has seen little children, extravagantly dressed and decorated, dancing in great hotel parlors on hot summer nights at an hour when they should all have been sound asleep in their beds, while their parents should have been soundly chastised for not putting them there. But is the dancing of young persons therefore wrong?

This is probably to the censorial mind nothing but the base compromise and sophistry of "moderate drinking." But nevertheless most of the evils of this kind are perversions of good things. There are a great many young and ignorant parents who become impatient with the incessant activity and restlessness of their children. They condemn them to sit still in a chair and make no noise. Dear madame, it is nature's intention that the child shall be restless, to develop his limbs. You apply to him rules that are fit and easy

43

for us who are old, and whom nature equally admonishes to sit still in chairs. Our little Procrustean beds are merely furniture that tortures. The desire of youth for enjoyment is as worthy as its desire for knowledge, for truth, for excellence. And it is the spirit, not the method, of enjoyments which are not obviously wrong, that is chiefly to be regarded. A good man asks whether he could go from dancing to console a dying bed. But could he go from skating, or reading Pickwick, or from heartily laughing, to console a dying friend? Would it not, even in his own view, depend wholly upon the mood in which he was doing it?

Let him select an act which he would approve. Let him be reading a serious book, or thinking in his study, or going upon a visit of charity when he is summoned, and he would say that he could go with perfect composure and the utmost propriety. But how if he were peevish as he read the serious book, or if he were thinking angrily in his study, or if he were mentally reproaching the duty that drew him from his comfortable room to pay a visit of charity, could he then more properly hasten to console the dying than if he had been cheerfully dancing, his mind full of pleasant thoughts and the delight of the music and the measured movement? It is not the thing that he is doing, but the spirit in which he is doing it, that should be considered.

How different a view of the pleasant recreation of dancing may be taken by an intellectual man, from that of one who thinks the waltz a device of Satan, is shown by a passage of De Quincey, the beginning of which the Easy Chair will quote, and which will find an echo in many a memory: "And in itself, of all the scenes which this world offers, none is to me so profoundly interesting, none (I say deliberately) so affecting, as the spectacle of men and women floating through the mazes of a dance; under these conditions, however, that the music shall be rich and festal, the execution of the dancers perfect, and the dance itself of a character to admit of free, fluent, and continuous action. And whenever the music happens not to be of a light, trivial character, but charged with the spirit of festal pleasure, and the performers in the dance so far skilful as to betray no awkwardness verging on the ludicrous, I believe that many persons feel as I feel in such circumstances, viz., derive from the spectacle the very grandest form of passionate sadness which can belong to any spectacle whatsoever."

THE HOG FAMILY

IT is a good sign of the times that the crusade against the large and omnipresent family of Hog which the Easy Chair long ago preached has been vigorously renewed. Public manners are a common interest. The private conduct of the most famous personages is of small concern beyond their domestic circle. But the conduct of the person in the next room at a hotel, or in the next seat in a railroad car, is of great interest to us. Yet the remedy is not obvious. Even if we should propose a school of manners, it is not certain that the pupils for whom it would be especially designed would attend.

If a fellow-guest at the Grand Hotel of the Universe comes in at two in the morning, and going humming along the corridor to his room, flings his boot down upon the floor at his door with a resounding blow that awakens all neighboring sleepers, you may cover him with expletives, and consign him in imagination to a hundred direful dooms, but nevertheless he goes unpunished. Or you may suddenly confront him in all the majesty of nocturnal dishabille, and admonish him severely of the wicked selfishness of his ways. But the probability is that you will have either an extremely amused audience, who will "guy" your appearance without mercy, or receive a surly rejoinder in the form of a boot or a volley of vituperation. In any event, the school of manners will not be honored by the exercises.

Yet the Hog family is not American, nor is it by any means peculiar to this country. The Lady Mavourneen who said with enthusiasm that she could travel without insult from the Atlantic to the Pacific, and that every American of the other sex seemed to make himself her protector, said only what is generally true of the American. He is naturally courteous and invincibly good-natured. Indeed, it is his good-nature which has permitted the family Hog to develop to such proportions. A man enters a hotel "as if it belonged to him." Will he not be forced to pay for his accommodation—and roundly? Shall he not take his ease in his inn? Is he not willing to settle for all the food, drink, comfort, trouble, that he may require or occasion? Shall he put himself out for others? If number one does not look out for itself, who will look out for it?

And to all this Jonathan good-naturedly assents. If number one takes more than his share of the sofa, Jonathan moves up. If number one puts his feet on a chair, Jonathan does not stare. If number one still more grossly demonstrates his porcine lineage, Jonathan dislikes to make trouble—until number one comes to despise those whom he insults, and plainly expects every circle to bow to the sovereignty of selfishness. This is a fatal form of good-nature, but it has a not unkindly origin. It springs from a social condition in which everybody is expected to help everybody else, because everybody needs help as in a frontier community. Indeed, in many a rural neighborhood still, this spirit of lending a hand is supreme. Everybody expects to submit to inconvenience, because he knows that he will require others to submit.

But these refinements of mutual dependence must not be allowed to justify the outrages of selfishness. The passenger in the boat or the train who occupies more than his seat, who sits in one chair, covers another with his feet, and a third with his bundles, and smokes, and widely squirts tobacco juice around him until his vicinity is not "a little heaven," but another kind of "h" below, is a public pest and general nuisance, for whose punishment there should be a common law of procedure. But this can be found only where there is a common contempt and resolution which will deprive him of his ill-gotten seats in the first place, and make him feel, in the second, the general scorn of his neighbors.

But as we are told constantly and correctly that we are a reading people, it is through reading that the members of the family which is hostis humani generis will learn that they are the most detestable and detested of the great families of the race. You, sir, whose eyes are skimming this page, and who never give your seat to a woman in the elevated car "on principle"—the principle being either that a woman ought not to get into a crowded car, knowing that she will put gentlemen to inconvenience; or that the company ought to forbid the entry of more passengers than there are seats; or that first come should be first served; or that number one, having paid for a seat, has a right to occupy it; or whatever other form the "principle" may assume—you are one of the host against whom the crusade is pushed. Thou art the—well, for the sake of euphony we will say man, but it is not man that is in the mind of your censors.

Or you, madam, who enter the railroad car with an air of right, and a look of reproval at every man who does not spring to his feet, and who settle yourself into the seat offered you without the least recognition of the courtesy that offers it—for you it would be well if the urbane mentor of another day were still here, who, having given his seat to a dashing young woman who seemed unconscious of his presence, looked at her until she impatiently demanded if he wanted anything, and he responding, said, blandly, "Yes, madam; I want to hear you say thank you."

Both this sir and madam may learn from the daily papers as from this page that even in a car where they recognize no acquaintance a cloud of witnesses around hold them in full survey, and whatever the fashion or richness of their garments, and however supercilious their air, perceive at once whether they belong to the family of ladies and gentlemen, or to that of Charles Lamb's "Mr. H." Thackeray's hero could not have been more aghast to see his divine Ottilia consume with gusto the oysters which were no longer fresh than Romeo to learn by his Juliet's question to that urbane mentor of other years that his mistress must be of kin to the unmentionable family.

The next time those boots are flung down in the reverberating hotel corridor there will be no harm in remarking to the clerk the next morning in the crowded office that it is not necessary for you to look upon the register to know that one of the Hog family arrived during the night.

THE ENLIGHTENED OBSERVER

THE Enlightened Observer from Europe who is studying American institutions asked the Easy Chair the other day what was meant by the statement that a candidate for a high elective office had opened headquarters in the neighborhood of a nominating convention. The Enlightened Observer said that he had always supposed that such conventions were assemblies which nominated persons whose public services and personal ability and character had distinguished them among their fellow-citizens, and shown them to be especially fitted for the offices which were to be filled. "Am I mistaken," he asked, "in supposing that to be the theory of your institutions?"

The Easy Chair could not say that he was, and conceded that such was the theory.

"In other words," continued the Enlightened Observer, "a republic secures good government because it intrusts the government not to the chance of birth, which may give to Oliver Cromwell a son Richard, and make the heir of Alexander the Great an Alexander the Little, but because it calls to its great offices of every degree those citizens who have demonstrated their peculiar fitness."

"That is certainly the theory of our republican institutions," returned the Easy Chair.

"Well?" said the Enlightened Observer.

"Well?" echoed the Easy Chair.

"Yes, but why, then, does a candidate open headquarters?"

"Yes, certainly. Why—that is—it is to make himself known."

"But the theory seems to assume that he is known already. Is it that he performs public services at the headquarters, or exhibits there his character and abilities? Is not the time a little limited and the space somewhat

49

inconvenient for such demonstrations? I am at a little loss. I can see that the personal appearance and manners of a candidate might be displayed favorably at a headquarters, and that, in a charming phrase of your country, he might dispense a generous hospitality in a hotel parlor, but how can he display his fitness for a high office in such narrow quarters as headquarters must be? Am I to understand that when Mr. John Jay was selected as a candidate for the Governorship of New York he had repaired previously to the place of nomination and had opened headquarters? Did General Washington pursue a similar course? If the services and character of a candidate have commended him to public favor and designated him as a suitable officer, why is not that enough?"

"Undoubtedly," answered the Easy Chair, "why isn't it? But I am afraid that you have not pursued your enlightened observations quite far enough, or you would have learned that in this country a kind providence is supposed to help those who help themselves, and that those who expect to have Governorships and Senatorships and other large and highly flavored political morsels offered to them on golden salvers and on bended knees will be seriously disappointed."

"I see," said, courteously, the Enlightened Observer, "that my excellent friend the Easy Chair is pleased to speak in metaphor. If I may penetrate it, he is declaring that great places are to be won like precious prizes, and do not drop into idle hands like fruit overripe. But if I may hold him to the point, is it not the theory of your institutions that it is services and character and ability that win the precious political prizes, and surely such qualities and services cannot be described as idle hands? I agree that providence helps those who help themselves, but who helps himself more than he who helps the entire community? And how does he help the community who opens headquarters to secure a prize for himself? Moreover, have I not heard that office should pursue the man, and not the man the office? Yet what is opening headquarters but pursuing office, as a hound a hare?"

The Easy Chair was obliged to suggest that there was no harm in knowing "the boys," and in showing the affability of a simple citizen "without airs," and making the acquaintance of important political personages, all of which the Enlightened Observer conceded, but still politely insisted that knowing the boys and showing affability and refraining from lofty demeanor did not demonstrate fitness for great place, and was a loss of proper personal dignity that ought not to be required of any one who had really approved himself as a suitable officer. He concluded that he might not have mistaken the theory, but he had certainly not apprehended the practice of our institutions.

"But surely," said the Easy Chair, "'tis but a small price to pay."

"True," said the Enlightened Observer, "it is a very small price; but I had not supposed that in the republic office was sold at any price. I thought that the good Santa Claus of public approval dropped it as a Christmas gift into the stocking of the most deserving. It seems, however, to be rather a raisin in snap-dragon—the prize of the toughest fingers."

RALPH WALDO EMERSON

THE beauty of Israel has fallen in its high place," said the voice of
Emerson's friend and neighbor, Judge Hoar, trembling and almost hushed
in emotion, and everybody who heard felt the singular felicity of the words.
The plain little country church was crowded, and a vast throng stood
outside in the peaceful April sunshine. Before the pulpit—the eyes forever
closed, the voice forever silent—lay the man whose aspect of sweet and
majestic serenity Death had not touched, and which recalled his own words:
"Even the corpse that has lain in the chambers has added a solemn
ornament to the house." It was the man who was beloved of his neighbors
and honored by the world, whose modest counsel in grave affairs guided
the village, and whose thought led the thought of Christendom. "He
belonged to all men, but he is peculiarly ours," said Judge Hoar truly,
speaking for the quiet historic town of which Emerson's grandfather had
been the minister, and in which he lived during the larger part of his life,
and to which his memory will lend an imperishable charm.

Concord when he first knew it was already famous. A hundred years ago, at
the bridge over the placid river, the Middlesex farmers, hastening as minute
men from all the neighboring country, had obeyed the first military
summons to fire upon the king's regulars; and the red-coated regulars,
turning, had begun, amid the blazing patriot volley of twenty miles, their
long retreat to Yorktown and over the sea. At the point where the highway
by which the soldiers marched enters the village, under the hill along whose
ridge the hurrying countrymen pressed to cut off the soldiers' retreat, lived
for more than forty years the scholar who belongs to Concord as
Shakespeare belongs to Stratford.

"Nature," said Emerson in his first book, written in the old Manse at
Concord, which Hawthorne afterwards inhabited, and which he has so

beautifully commemorated—"Nature stretcheth out her arms to embrace man: only let his thoughts be of equal greatness. Willingly does she follow his steps with the rose and the violet, and bend her lines of grandeur and grace to the decoration of her darling child. Only let his thoughts be of equal scope, and the frame will suit the picture. A virtuous man is in unison with her works, and makes the central figure of the visible sphere. Homer, Pindar, Socrates, Phocion, associate themselves fitly in our memory with the geography and climate of Greece. The visible heavens and the earth sympathize with Jesus. And in common life whoever has seen a person of powerful character and happy genius will have remarked how easily he took all things along with him, the persons, the opinions, and the day, and nature became auxiliary to a man." So is Emerson associated with the tranquil landscape of the old Middlesex town—the gentle hills, the long sweep of meadowland, the winding river, the woodland, and the pastures under the ample sky. The broad horizon and rural repose were the fitting home of the lofty and beneficent genius whose life and word perpetually illustrated the supreme worth and beauty of truth, purity, and morality. Whoever saw him there or elsewhere, saw the "sweet and virtuous soul" which George Herbert likened to seasoned timber that never gives.

The sincerity and serenity of Emerson's character were unsurpassed. The freshness and glow of his interest in life were perennial. With a sober tenderness of regret he said to a friend who congratulated him upon his seventieth birthday, "Yet it is a little sad to me, for I count to-day the end of youth." In no other sense than the lapse of years, however, was it true. That auroral freshness of soul which is the distinctive charm of youth lingered when even memory somewhat failed. "How long it is since I have seen you!" he said at Longfellow's funeral to a friend whom he had accosted just before. But he said it with all that heartiness of sympathy and expectation which, in the golden prime of his life, when he was in many ways the most striking and original figure in his country, made him greet every comer as if he expected to hear from him a wiser word than had yet been spoken. A youth, fascinated by this simple graciousness of manner, declared that Emerson greeted the most ordinary persons like a King of Spain receiving an ambassador from the Great Mogul. The expectancy of his manner implied that every man had some message to deliver, and he bent himself to hear.

But his shrewdness of perception was exquisite. He did not take dross because he hoped for gold. His reproof was as sure and incisive as the stroke of a delicate Damascus blade. When a young man, hearing Emerson say that everybody ought to read Plato, followed his advice, and read, he thought, with the audacity of youth, that he detected faults in Plato, and wrote an essay to set them forth. He asked Emerson to read it, and when he returned it to the youth, Emerson said, pleasantly, "My boy, when you strike at the king, you must kill him." One day he sat at dinner with a distinguished company of statesmen. He was by far the most famous man at the table; but he modestly followed the conversation, turning from each guest who spoke, to the next, with the old sweet gravity of earnest expectation. When all the notable company had gone, a guest who remained said to him: "I saw you talking with the English Minister. He is a brilliant man, and I hope that you found him agreeable." "A very pleasant gentleman," replied Emerson; "but he does not represent the England that I know."

Despite this sharp apprehension, however, Emerson was sometimes unable to find any charm in writings which have apparently taken a permanent place in literature. He could see nothing interesting or valuable in Shelley. "When I read Shelley," he once said, "I am like a man who thinks that he sees gold at the bottom of a stream. He reaches for it, but his hands come up cold, with a little common sand in them." The waywardness and disorder of Shelley's life may have troubled him. But this would not have affected his intellectual judgment. His acute intellect was supremely independent and absolutely courageous. "He must embrace solitude as a bride," he said of the scholar; "he must have his glees and his glooms alone." When as a young man he quietly closed his pulpit door, and declined to preach any more, because he no longer felt any value in certain religious rites, there was no protest, nor ostentation, nor newspaper "sensation." It was simply the closing of a book that he had read, and the amazement and censure and grief of others could not possibly persuade him to do, or to say, or to affect, the thing that was not true. Emerson's moral and intellectual integrity was transparently simple, but it was sublime. It was not expressed in stormy self-assertion nor cynical contempt. It spoke in tranquil and beautiful affirmation, perfectly courteous, but absolutely sincere.

But no man more charitably and diligently sought to understand others, and to be just to what was obscure and foreign to him. He listened patiently to music. But it did not charm him. He was punctual in the duties of a citizen. But he had no proper political tastes. Yet for the true politics, the application of the moral law to the control of public affairs, no man was more perceptive or uncompromising. He was always on the right side of great public questions. His hospitable sympathy entertained every good cause, and in all our antislavery literature there is no nobler or more permanent work than his address upon the anniversary of West India emancipation in 1844. The only cloud that ever arose upon his regard for Carlyle was his displeasure with Carlyle's contemptuous and cynical sneers at our civil war. He was deeply impatient of doubtful and half-hearted Americans during the war. "They call themselves gentlemen, I believe," he said of certain persons, and in a tone which showed that his lofty and patriotic honor instinctively and utterly repudiated the pinchbeck claims of educated feebleness to bear "the grand old name of gentleman."

Those who recall Emerson when he was a clergyman in Boston remember a singular spiritual beauty in the man, and an indescribable charm of manner in his public speech. But apparently he impressed his earlier associates with the purity and refinement of his mind and life, his lofty intellectual tastes and sympathy, and his literary accomplishment, rather than by the peculiar force of a genius which was to give the most powerful spiritual impulse of the generation to American thought. This is the more singular because there was always something breezy and heroic in his tone, which might have led to the suspicion of the fact that he was from the first a fond reader of Plutarch, from whose "Lives" he draws so many illustrations. As in a mountain walk the traveller is suddenly aware of wafts of perfumed air, now of the wild-grape blossom, now of the azalea or sweet-brier, so the strain of Emerson suggests his sympathy with Plutarch and Montaigne, the Oriental poets and the Platonists.

But no one could describe accurately his "system" of philosophy, nor fit him into a "school" of poetry. He was content to call himself a scholar, and no name was more significant and precious to him. He shunned notoriety, but he had the instinctive desire of every artist and of all genius for an audience. When a friend asked him of a young man whose literary talent had seemed to him to promise great achievement, Emerson said: "He does nothing; and I doubted his genius when I saw that he did not seek a hearing." When his own first slight volume, "Nature," was published, they were but a few, a very few, who perceived in it the ripe and beautiful work of a master in literature and thought. The richness and originality and picturesque simplicity of this book, its subtle perception, its tone of jubilant power, and the soft glimmering light of lofty imagination which irradiates every page, do not lose by familiarity, and are as charming, although of course not so surprising, as when they first took captive the readers of nearly fifty years ago. With the eagerness of classification which characterizes many active minds, Emerson was immediately labelled a Berkeleyan, an idealist, and a mystic. But he eluded the precise classification as noiselessly and surely as a cloud changes its form. Astonishment, satire, indignation, contradiction, spent themselves in vain. Like a rose-tree in June, which blossoms sweetly whether the air be chilly or sunny, his thought quietly flowered into exquisite expression. You might like it or leave it. But the rose would be still a rose.

There was a fashion of calling Emerson obscure. But there is no style in literature of more poetic precision than his. It is full of surprises of beauty and aptness. His central doctrine of the identity of men, the grandeur of every man's opportunity, and the essential poetry of the circumstances of common life, was a living faith. "The great man," he said, "makes the great thing." "In the sighing of these woods; in the quiet of these gray fields; in the cool breeze that sings out of these Northern mountains; in the workmen, the boys, the maidens you meet; in the hopes of the morning, the ennui of noon, and sauntering of the afternoon; in the disquieting comparisons; in the regrets at want of vigor; in the great idea and the puny execution—behold Charles the Fifth's day; another, yet the same; behold Chatham's, Hampden's, Bayard's, Alfred's, Scipio's, Pericles's day—day of all that are born of women. The difference of circumstance is merely costume. I am tasting the self-same life—its sweetness, its greatness, its pain—which I so admire in other men." The temptation to complete the splendid passage is almost irresistible. But in every page you are drawn on as in a stately symphony of winning music.

This passage is from the Dartmouth College address, and it has all the flowing cadence of a discourse written to be spoken. Yet Emerson had little of the orator's temperament save the desire of an audience, and an earnestness which was pure and not passionate. But no orator in the country has exercised a deeper or more permanent influence. His discourses were but essays, but their thought was so noble, their form so symmetrical, their tone so lofty, and they were spoken with such alluring rhythm, that they threw over young minds a spell which no other eloquence could command. Emerson himself was very susceptible to the power of fine oratory. No man ever praised more warmly the charm of Everett in his earlier day. When Webster delivered his eulogy upon Adams and Jefferson in Faneuil Hall, Emerson was teaching in Cambridge, and Richard H. Dana, Jun., was one of his pupils. The day before Webster spoke, the teacher announced that there would be no school upon the morrow, and he earnestly exhorted his pupils not to lose the memorable opportunity of hearing the great orator. Dana was of an age to prefer fishing to oratory, and strolled off with his line to the river, where he passed the day. When school was resumed, Mr. Emerson with sympathetic interest asked him if he had heard Webster. The fisher, half ashamed, reluctantly owned his absence. Emerson looked at him with regret and almost pain, and said to him, gravely: "My boy, I am very sorry; you have lost what you can never recover, and what you will regret to the last day of your life."

But those who heard his own Divinity School address, or the Cambridge or Dartmouth oration, or the Emancipation address, would not exchange that recollection even to have heard the Olympian orator in Faneuil Hall. "Tell me," said a Senator famous for his oratory, to a friend in Washington, "what do you call eloquence? Repeat to me an eloquent passage." The friend quoted from Emerson the unequalled passage from the Dartmouth College address in which the scholar appeals to the young men to be true to the ideals of their youth—a passage which no generous youth can read to-day without deep emotion and a thrill of high resolve. The Senator listened with an air of perplexed incredulity. "Do you call that eloquent? Now see what I call eloquence," and he declaimed a glowing piece of rhetoric with ardent feeling. It was a passage from Charles Sprague's Fourth-of-July oration in Boston sixty years ago. But effective as it was, his friend reminded the Senator that if the test of eloquence be glow of feeling and splendor and sincerity of expression, with an inner power of appeal which searches the heart and moulds the life, no really greater results in this country could be traced to any speech than to that of Emerson, who read the greater part of his essays as addresses, and who sometimes reached a lyrical strain which not the magnificent Burke nor any other great orator surpasses.

—To talk of Emerson, even if the talker were not of the circle of his intimate friends, is to raise the flood-gate of happy and inspiring recollections. It is one of the tenderest of the thoughts that hover around his memory, as the low winds sigh through the pine-trees over his grave, that, as with Longfellow, there are no excuses to be made for grotesque eccentricities of genius, nor for a life at any point unworthy of so great a soul. He said of his friend Thoreau, who is buried near him, that he was like the Alpine climber who gathers the edelweiss, the flower that blooms at the very edge of the glacier. He too lived at those pure heights, and taught us how to tread them undazzled and undismayed. Happy teacher, whose long and lovely life illustrated the dignity and excellence of the truth, old as the morning and as ever fresh, that fidelity to the divine law written upon the conscience is the only safe law of life for every man. Noble and beneficent preacher, who, in a sense that the pensive Goldsmith did not intend,
"Allured to brighter worlds, and led the way."

HENRY WARD BEECHER

FOR forty years Mr. Beecher had been minister of Plymouth Church when on a Sunday morning suddenly came the news that his ministry and probably his life were ended; and he died a day or two afterwards. The preacher and the church were more widely known than any others in the Union, and during all his pastorate he was one of the most conspicuous figures in the country. He was undoubtedly also one of the most famous preachers of his time and of the English race, and the death of Wendell Phillips left him the most eminent of American orators. There have been popular preachers during Mr. Beecher's career, like Moffit and other revivalists, and there are always eloquent and scholarly orators in the American pulpit. The tradition of Summerfield presents a beautiful youth and a captivating speaker. The charm of Channing was profound and indescribable. But Beecher recalls Whitefield more than any other renowned preacher. Like Whitefield, he was what is known as a man of the people; a man of strong virility, of exuberant vitality, of quick sympathy, of an abounding humor, of a rapid play of poetic imagination, of great fluency of speech; an emotional nature overflowing in ardent expression, of strong convictions, of complete self-confidence; but also not sensitive, nor critical, nor judicial; a hearty, joyous nature, touching ordinary human life at every point, and responsive to every generous moral impulse.

Mr. Beecher was not a pioneer, nor a leader of forlorn hopes, but of the main column of the army. He marched just ahead of the advance, and touched with his elbows those who moved forward with him. He liked to feel the warmth of their breath upon his cheek, and the magnetism of their neighborhood. He spoke for them as they could not speak for themselves. He liked the crowd. The hum and throb of multitudinous life inspired and cheered him. He was at home in streets and towns; with a bright jest for

59

every comer; a happy quip and repartee; with an eye and a heart for the unfortunate and forlorn, and a ready rebuke for insolence and injustice. He had nothing of the recluse or scholarly habit; no fastidious taste. He was fond of pictures and music and all forms of art, without especial aesthetic accomplishment; a man of cheery presence, of cordial address; with a willing word for the reporter, chaffing the interviewer; jumping on the street-car in motion; yet always seemly, and always, despite his slouched hat and careless dress, undeniably clerical, but with no undue professional sense of dignity or decorum.

In the pulpit, or, more truly, upon the platform—for whether preaching, or lecturing, or speaking at table or upon the stump, he seemed to be always upon the platform—he inculcated right living rather than traditional doctrine. He was a soldier of the church militant, but his warfare was with human wrong and misery, and false theories of life, and low aims and poor ambitions. He aimed to build up righteousness of life, and in the ardor of the strife he liked to pause and wink, and let fly a bright-tipped, winged word at the opponent, against whom he bore no kind of malice. He hated the wrong, but not the wrong-doer. Ardent and impulsive, his generous emotions often overwhelmed his judgment; and in politics, although the most popular of stump-orators, and never happier or more truly himself than in a political speech, in which, with the instinct of a born fighter, he "drank delight of battle," yet he sometimes amazed and confounded his friends, who, however, could not doubt his sincerity nor question his purpose.

The great cloud that fell upon his life seemed also to darken the country. The grief and consternation showed how strong a hold he had upon the national mind and heart, which indeed was never so firm as at the very moment that his good name seemed to be obscured. It was the most tremendous ordeal to which any public man of his peculiar character and quality of eminence has ever been exposed in this country. The most remarkable fact in it all was the way in which he endured it. The blacker the cloud appeared to be, the more sturdy was his stern defiance, and for weeks of seemingly accumulating and insurmountable obstruction he faced unflinchingly a possible doom the mere prospect of which might well have withered a brave heart conscious of innocence. That the cloud ever wholly disappeared cannot be said, in view of the tone of the press even as he lay dead in his house. But that he could never have maintained his position as he did if he had not been generally acquitted in the public mind seems to be indisputable. If the relation of his later life to the country was somewhat changed, the result was due to the decline of confidence in what had been believed to be his strongest quality, supreme good sense and sound judgment, rather than to doubt of his moral integrity.

No man lived more in the public eye and for the public than Mr. Beecher.

In his speeches and sermons and writings he took the public into his confidence with a freedom that was characteristic and natural in him, but which would have been extraordinary in any other man. He could not pass through the street without universal recognition, and no man in the two cities was so well known to everybody as he. At public meetings and at dinners where he was to speak, he came late amid smiling and expectant applause, and with the air of saying, "Where MacGregor sits, there is the head of the table." He had the right to that air, for wherever he was to speak he was the chief orator. But he was no niggard of generous praise and sympathy, and no man spoke with more fervent eulogy and eloquent approval of other men. Doubtless, like an actor or singer, the long habit of receiving applause had made it pleasant to him, and as is the fact with all extempore speaking, the greater the applause the higher the eloquence of his strain. It is a reciprocal action. Of Mr. Beecher's later platform speeches, the most remarkable was his political address at the Brooklyn Rink in 1884, which was delivered amid a storm of enthusiasm, while in the delivery he was himself wrought to the highest feeling.

His power over the emotions of an audience was unsurpassed in this country probably since Patrick Henry. Thomas Corwin and Sergeant Prentiss perhaps were as great masters of humor and patriotic appeal upon the stump; but Beecher added to these a pathos and sentiment and poetic tone in which the others did not excel. He had not the fine, glittering, incisive touch of Wendell Phillips's fatal sarcasm and vituperation. Phillips stood quietly and played his polished rapier with a flexible wrist, but its point was deadly; Beecher smote, and crushed. One was the deft Saladin with his chased and curving cimeter, the other was Richard with his heavy battle-axe. In the great controversy in which both were engaged, upon the same side, indeed, but under different banners and wearing different colors, Beecher and Phillips, amid a chorus of eloquence, were the two chief voices. Garrison was not distinctively an orator, while Phillips was the especial and distinctive orator of the cause, and his fame as a public man belongs to that cause alone. But Beecher had many interests and relations, and his oratory had other strains. They were friends always, and Phillips spoke often in Plymouth Church, and uttered many a glowing word of his fellow-laborer.

When these words are published the freshness of the impression of Beecher's death will have passed, and from every part of the country his eulogy will have been spoken. The universal emotion, the warmth and tenor of the tributes, will have shown how eminent a figure he was, and that his death is felt to be a national loss. One of the papers described him as the last of a great generation, and Senator Cullom, speaking of Logan in the crowded Brooklyn Academy on the evening of Beecher's death, called a roll of illustrious names, of which his was the latest, and among which it surely belongs. His profession was the preaching of peace and good-will. But how often he must have felt that his Master came not to bring peace, but a sword! His buoyant temperament, his perfect health, his love of nature and of man, of children and flowers, of the changing sky and landscape, his abounding sympathy, his rich and sensitive humor, made his life joyous and often happy. But it was none the less a stormy life, ending at last, amid the sorrow of a country, in happy rest and the good fame of a great orator for human welfare.

THE GOLDEN AGE

IN this country we are inclined to believe that the epoch that followed the Revolution was one of the utmost purity and simplicity. But it was one of the "fathers" who said to a friend upon the adjournment of the first Congress, "Do you suppose such a set of rascals will ever assemble again?" In his diary John Adams appeals to the calmer mind and juster judgment of the coming age—meaning that in which we live, and from which we look wistfully back to old John Adams's cocked hat and knee-breeches as the symbols of a nobler time.

Then there is Fisher Ames, one of the famous orators and conspicuous leaders of the beginning of the century, who, studying his country at the time to which we recur as the age of high purpose and lofty men, bewails the sordidness, selfishness, and degradation around him. "Of course," he says, seventy years ago, "the single passion that engrosses us, the only avenue to consideration and importance in our society, is the accumulation of property: our inclinations cling to gold, and are bedded in it as deeply as that precious ore in the mine.... As experience evinces that popularity—in other words, consideration and power—is to be procured by the meanest of mankind, the meanest in spirit and understanding, and in the worst of ways, it is obvious that at present the incitement to genius is next to nothing."

We might suppose that we were listening to a contemporary cynic; and whoever reads the history of the politics of that time will find that "the better days of the republic" were very like the days in which we deplore their disappearance. When Mr. Ames died, Mr. John Quincy Adams wrote a review of his works, in which, with the equanimity and moderation of the golden age, he remarks, "It is a melancholy contemplation of human nature to see a mind so highly cultivated and so richly gifted as that of Mr. Ames soured and exasperated into the very ravings of a bedlamite." He then proceeds to speak of those who, without believing Mr. Ames's "absurd and inconsistent political creed," are selfishly eager for its propagation, being "choice spirits, amounting to at most six hundred" (their name was the Essex Junto!), and who hold that "the porcelain must rule over the earthenware, the blind and sordid multitude must put themselves, bound hand and foot, into the custody of the lynx-eyed, seraphic souls of the six hundred, and then all together must go and squat for protection under the hundred hands of the British Briareus."

To this gentle strain Mr. John Lowell replied in a similar vein, beginning by speaking of the malignity of Mr. Adams's sarcasm, and of his following Mr. Ames to the grave with crocodile tears, informing him that he had no need to assail Mr. Ames's friends with all the venom of an infuriated partisan, because he had already obtained his reward for "ratting" from the Federalists, and this act of gratitude to his benefactors was unnecessary. Mr. Lowell ends his reply by saying that in the course of a short political life Mr. Adams had received more than seventy thousand dollars from the public, and that while no man pitied Mr. Ames, "Mr. Adams is an object of sincere commiseration with many a man of high and honorable feelings, while it is to be doubted whether he is the object of envy to any man on earth."

These are glimpses of the golden age, of that "better day" of the republic with which our own is so often and so injuriously contrasted. Indeed, there is no finer cordial for despondency than a glance at the paradise that hovers behind our retreating steps. The mountain traveller turns and sees a lovely vision floating in the sky.

"How faintly flushed, how phantom-fair,
Was Monte Rosa, hanging there—
A thousand shadowy-pencil'd valleys,
And snowy dells in a golden air."

Good lack! he cries, are those the crags and precipices along which I slid and stumbled in terror of my life? The hanging gardens of the past, the halcyon epoch of our history, the lost paradise of our fathers, are all crags and precipices along which the race and our country have stumbled and slid. If any man is disposed to think that he has fallen upon evil times, let him open his history. It is a marvellous tonic.

Does he think republics ungrateful? Look at Mr. Motley's vivid portrait of John of Barneveld. When he was seventy-two years old he writes from his prison to his wife and family: "I receive at this moment the very heavy and sorrowful tidings that I, an old man, for all my services done well and faithfully to the fatherland for so many years ... must prepare myself to die to-morrow." Does he think irreligion undermining society? Look into Smiles's "Huguenots in France after the Revocation of the Edict of Nantes." For attending Huguenot meetings men were captured by soldiers and sentenced to the galleys, mostly for life. They were chained by the neck with murderers and other criminals, and were quartered in Paris in the dungeon of the Chateau de la Tournelle. Thick iron collars were attached by iron chains to the beams. The collar was closed around the prisoner's neck, and riveted with blows of a hammer upon an anvil. Twenty men in pairs were chained to each beam. They could not sleep lying; they could not sleep sitting or standing up straight, for the beam was too high for the one and too low for the other. This was done in the name of religion. The age of Louis the Fourteenth is called one of the great epochs of the world. It was an age in which the king's mistress persuaded him to slaughter and banish hundreds of thousands of his subjects because of their religious faith, and the great preachers of his church applauded, and the Holy Father approved, and even Madame de Sévigné, whose letters some young ladies at Newport and Saratoga are diligently reading, and sighing for the good old witty times in which she lived, wrote of the most innocent and most devoted men: "Hanging is quite a refreshment to me. They have just taken twenty-four or thirty of these men, and are going to throw them off."

The golden age is not yesterday or to-morrow, but to-day. It is the age in which we live, not that in which somebody else lived. The trouble, vexation, corruption, weakness, selfishness, meanness, which dismay us and tempt us to despair are the old lions that have always beset the path. No man is born out of time; and what man living to-day, who is not pinched with poverty or disease, would have lived a thousand years ago? If our politics seem mean and our men small, how does Alfred's time seem, or the glory of Athens, or the court of Louis the Fourteenth, or Luther's Germany? What did Jefferson think of Hamilton, or the Aurora say of Washington?

SPRING PICTURES

IN a late beautiful spring afternoon the Easy Chair rolled itself into the suburbs for a stroll. There were everywhere the signs of the advance of a great city and the pathetic forlornness of the municipal frontier. Pleasant country-houses, spacious, rambling, with broad piazzas and gardens and lawns, had been apparently suddenly overtaken by streets and stone sidewalks and lamps. There were the rattle and shriek of the incessant railway trains near by. Tall factory chimneys smoked and machinery hummed and steam-whistles blew all around the quiet old houses. The contrast gave them a kind of conscious life. They seemed to be aware of the incongruity of their character with the new neighborhood. They had a helpless air, as if nothing remained but submission to division into regular building lots and the absolute extinction of rural seclusion and charm. There was the impression of a faint and futile struggle between city and country, in which, indeed, for a moment the excellence of each was lost, but the result of which was not doubtful.

As the Easy Chair pushed on, it saw in fancy the old pastoral peace and retirement of the places when they were indeed in the country. It recalled the noted men of that older day who sought here relaxation and repose. There was the placid river, on which no restless steamer foamed, but only silent sloops drifted or careened. Yonder were the leafy coves under the wooded and rocky banks, from which the Indian had but recently paddled his canoe. No railroad harmed the virgin shyness of the shore. It was El Dorado, Arcadia, the land of Goshen. It was the home of peace, of plenty, of content.

Such a poet, such a painter, is idealizing memory on a spring afternoon in the suburbs. It seemed so gross a wrong that sidewalks and gas lamps and factory chimneys and steam-whistles should invade and devastate the tranquil fields that indignant imagination filled them as fact with all the fancies that tranquil fields suggest. Doubtless in the closets of those quiet houses there were the bones of plenty of old skeletons. Those spacious, sunny rooms were the scenes of the familiar domestic tragedies against which not the most romantic of country-houses can shut the door. Up those steps have swayed and hesitated the doubtful feet of the oldest son, heir of precious hopes and child of fervent prayers, hesitating and lingering at hours long past midnight, watched for and waited for by the mother's heart that breaks but does not falter. In that broad hall, on the brightest of May mornings, the daughter of the house has stood, radiant as the day, and crowned with orange blossoms. There have met the hopes and joys of youth, the tears and blessings and farewells of older years. The pretty pageant filled the house, and faded slowly and utterly away. The old house has known, too, the solemn shadow that falls on every house. It seems to regretful memory the abode of unchanging delight. But from that door the slow procession moved, and those whose hospitable smile and word had hallowed every room returned no more. They are gone, the bride, the parent, the friend; "they are all gone, the old familiar faces," the age, the society, the politics, the interests. They are all gone. Why should not the house go too?

It was early spring, and the Easy Chair, looking up, saw half a dozen kites flying in the air. A little further, and laughing girls were skipping rope. Boys were spinning peg-tops and playing marbles and driving hoops. The boys and girls who lived in the quiet old country-house did the same a hundred years ago. They flew kites and drove hoops, and that little bride skipped rope and carried dolls. The age, the society, the politics, the interests, were very different. They are, indeed, all changed. But tops are changeless, marbles are immortal, and so are boys and girls. They know nothing of the old house over which the Easy Chair becomes pensive. They belong to the new time, which demands its demolition.

PROPER AND IMPROPER

LONGFELLOW has commemorated in a beautiful sonnet the delightful evenings of Mrs. Kemble's readings; and certainly it was a singular pleasure to see and to hear her. Her historic name associated her with her uncle John and her aunt Mrs. Siddons, and she had always the port of one conscious of a famous lineage. She used to say, with a half-humorous, half-proud emphasis, that she belonged to her majesty's players, and in her presence it was easy to believe that her majesty's players were an important body in the state. Her power of identification with the various characters in the plays, and the skill with which she maintained the individuality throughout, were always remarkable, and the symmetry and completeness of the whole performance left nothing to be criticised. The only observation that suggested itself might be that the stage traditions were evident in her rendering. But that, in turn, only suggested the further question whether the traditions were not worthy of respect. Dramatic and histrionic forms of art, like all others, are but representations of nature under certain conditions and limitations. They are not an imitation, a fac-simile, and every man will be at odds with any work of art in any kind who does not bear this in mind.

The spectator complains of unnaturalness upon the stage; the substance of his feeling is that people do not talk and act so in ordinary life. That is true; but if the theatre should show us men and women doing upon the stage what they do in ordinary life, the theatre would be no more attractive than the street or the parlor. It is not the spectacle of ordinary life that we expect to see in the theatre. It is a view of human life and nature under ideal conditions, and it is as irrelevant to require that the player shall seem to us like the man with whom we have been transacting business as that he should speak plain prose instead of blank verse. If Mrs. Kemble had read the words of Rosalind or of Portia, of Shylock or Mercutio, as if they were

69

neighbors of hers and people whom we were in the habit of meeting, the effect would have been ludicrous. When she came in—the Fanny Kemble of Talfourd and of the wild enthusiasm of the grandfathers of to-day, ripened into the comely and queenly woman—and seated herself at the little table on which the great volume lay open, she was the magician who was to open to us the realm of faery, the world of imagination, not to take us back into the familiar scenes of the world of New York or Chicago. The spell was resistless. The deep, rich, melodious voice flowed out like an enchanted singing river, along which we glided seeing visions and dreaming dreams. To sit and listen to her was like sitting and watching Titian laying on the canvas the gorgeous tints which before our eyes took on the forms of men and angels. A rarer, a more refined delight, which of us has known? Did it ever occur to us that Mrs. Kemble was doing anything improper, anything unwomanly? In the wonderful picture of Portia that "her voice's music" drew, was there anything a little repulsive, a little unfeminine?

This question was suggested to the Easy Chair by the remark of one of the most devoted and delighted of all the listeners at those readings, that he was very sorry to see that the University of London had decided to admit women to all its degrees upon precisely equal terms with men. The secret reason of the regret, of course, is the feeling that there would be something unwomanly in the act of competing for a degree which would open the pursuit of professions—especially the medical profession—which are usually and often exclusively cultivated by men.

Yet, when pressed, the Easy Chair's interlocutor admitted that there was nothing more essentially unfeminine in the practice of medicine by a woman than in the recitation of Shakespeare for the entertainment of a miscellaneous crowd. It is a question of habit, not of instinct, nor of principle, nor of reason. When the old Greek and Oriental idea of absolute seclusion and subordination is abandoned, a woman's reading from Shakespeare for the pleasure of the public is an action not different in kind from her practising medicine or serving on a school committee. This generation, however, is more used to the one than to the other. It is a habit, nothing more.

Charles Lamb regrets in one of his later essays that "we have no rationale of sauces, or theory of mixed flavors; as to show why cabbage is reprehensible with roast beef, laudable with bacon; why the haunch of mutton seeks the alliance of currant jelly, the shoulder civilly declineth it; why loin of veal (a pretty problem), being itself unctuous, seeketh the adventitious lubricity of melted butter; and why the same part in pork, not more oleaginous, abhorreth from it; ... why oysters in death rise up against the contamination of brown sugar, while they are posthumously amorous of vinegar; why the sour mango and the sweet jam by turns court and are accepted by the compilable mutton hash—she not yet decidedly declaring for either. We are as yet but in the empirical stage of cookery."

It is not in cookery alone that this mystery is still unsolved. Why, for instance, should it seem a womanly use of Heaven's gift that Jenny Lind should sing for the pleasure of a thousand men, and something strange and unfeminine that Portia should plead with eloquence in a court to save a hapless woman from prison or the cord? Why is it fitting that Mrs. Kemble should professionally read Shakespeare, and "queer" that she should professionally attend women in peril and sickness? Do we not naturally and logically glide into the part of the citation from Lamb that we just now omitted?—"why salmon (a strong sapor per se) fortifieth its condition with the mighty lobster sauce, whose embraces are fatal to the delicater relish of the turbot." Must we not say that we are as yet but in the rudimentary knowledge of what is and is not feminine?

When the example of the London University is not singular, but when all opportunities are opened equally to all talent and vocation, when it is not forbidden a woman to do any honorable work for which she is by nature and by study and training properly equipped, unless the laws of nature fail, will any greater catastrophe befall, will there be any more signal reversion of the order of things, than if cabbage should come at last to be eaten with roast beef, and currant jelly cement an alliance with the mutton's shoulder?

BELINDA AND THE VULGAR

IT is perhaps because the Easy Chair sometimes discusses questions of behavior that it is occasionally asked to express an opinion upon more difficult social points. Thus it was lately requested to say whether it did not think that the great want of our society is a social standard. The inquiry was made by the lovely Belinda, who was charmingly dressed for a select party, and the Easy Chair was obliged to own that it did not at once comprehend the scope of the inquiry, and to seek an explanation. As Belinda proceeded to elucidate her meaning it seemed to be tolerably plain that she was contemplating some kind of rank, or visible and recognized distinction, which should separate "society" from what is not society, and it was impossible not to feel that, however high the dividing line, and however small the circle which it enclosed, she was herself included within it.

The Easy Chair thereupon described to her a conversation which it held long ago with a distinguished man upon English social life and the advantages of an aristocracy. The distinguished man's views were very much like those which are set forth in Disraeli's "Sibyl" and "Coningsby," and which were known forty years ago as those of Young England. They proposed a national life blended of feudal romance and modern philanthropy. There was to be a gracious nobility of very blue blood which had been clarified in the veins of the Plantagenets, who were to live in stately castles in the midst of superb demesnes, and to be exceedingly good to their tenants and retainers, for whom there were to be May-poles, and flitches of bacon at Christmas, and greased poles to climb at appropriate times, and sacks to run races in, and who were to be visited at their neat little cottages, when they were ill, by the ladies from the castle, and who were to be industrious and obedient and humble and grateful, and, above all things, to know their place. The nobility were to own the land, and govern the country, and live in splendid idleness, and the happy peasantry were to do all the work, and bow respectfully when the nobility passed by, and go to bed when the curfew tolled, and to make no trouble.

This was the Young England programme, and the Arcadia of the Disraeli novel. And this also showed its familiar features in the talk of the distinguished man as he bewailed the social bareness of American life and descanted upon the charm of an ancient and well-ordered society. But when the Easy Chair mischievously asked him whether he did not think that he might tire of the greased pole, and the dance upon the lawn, and the gracious patronage, and the respectful gratitude, the amusing bewilderment of the distinguished man showed that in his admiration of the society that he described he assumed always that he was to belong to the class that lived in the stately castles and benignly condescended to the humble cottagers. His view, therefore, was very simple. It was merely that he should like to live in splendid idleness, steeped in luxury, and surrounded by respectful servants.

Belinda listened to this story, of which the Easy Chair made no application, with a slight blush; and to the polite inquiry, what kind of social standard she contemplated, she responded that she meant a certain fixed line which should exclude the vulgar. But she was immediately silent, as if reflecting upon a difficult proposition, and did not answer when she was asked what she thought would be the consequence of removing the vulgar from the circles which she considered most select.

Her benevolent attention invited further question, especially as at the same moment a lady entered the room who bore one of the most noted family names in the country, and most familiar in fashionable annals, a family which delights to trace its lineage to a royal source. This proud dame had married her daughter as if by main force to a coroneted lord of hereditary acres. It was a familiar fact of the society in which she was a conspicuous figure, and it was impossible not to ask: "Can there be anything more coarsely vulgar than to sell a daughter for money and a title to a man for whom she does not care; and shall we begin to erect the social standard by expelling the vulgar offender?"

Belinda was still silent, and the brilliant rooms began to fill and murmur with a gay company. Among them came the loud and diamonded Mrs. Smasher, to whose unparalleled fêtes even Belinda would be almost willing to request a card. The Smasher lineage is not renowned or regal; the Smasher mind is imperfectly educated; the Smasher manners are those of the suddenly rich who are not also suddenly refined.

"Is any conceivable vulgarity greater than the Smasher vulgarity, O Belinda; and shall we continue these exercises by expelling also this essentially vulgar person?"

Belinda was still silent. She has remained silent even to this day.

DECAYED GENTILITY

DECAYED gentility has great interest for the novel-reader, and the man and woman who "have seen better days" are familiar figures in actual life. Hampton Court is regarded by some travellers with pensive regard as a kind of almshouse for this class of the indigent, and institutions nearer home are described with a deferential courtesy and avoidance as homes for decayed gentlewomen. It cannot be pleasant to the persons themselves to be so described, but the founders of such places have perhaps a comfortable sense of reflected honor, as if the impulse to provide a retreat of the kind were of itself a sign of "very gentility." Despite the plaintive little plea which the description itself urges for this decayed class of our fellow-beings, the people who "have seen better days" are not generally an engaging multitude. A person whose chief distinction is that he was once more prosperous than he is now seems to renounce any present claim upon consideration, and to offer his inability as a ground of regard. It is an appeal to pity, but pity of old has a disagreeable relative.

The pathos of the appeal lies, first, in the sense of contrast, and then in the spiritual rather than the material poverty which it discloses. The lady who lets lodgings, and whose air and the allusions of whose conversation constantly suggest that she has seen better days, is a person who is mastered by circumstances, and therefore does not compel respect. But a woman who is the perfectly self-respecting lady fulfils simply the duty of the moment with no conscious appeal for sympathy; and if by chance you discover that she has been more prosperous, the fact that she has not the conceit of it strengthens your regard. For it is no personal credit to have been more prosperous. As your landlady shows you the convenience of the room, she lets fall that her father the Bishop, or her uncle the Senator, or her lamented cousin the millionaire would be deeply grieved if he could know that his kinswoman was actually letting lodgings.

"Then, madam, you have seen better days?"

"Ah, sir—"

But how is it personally creditable to the good woman that her uncle was honorable and her cousin rich? She recalls the circumstances of others at the expense of her own character. The lodger wishes to hire rooms upon their own merits. He resents the bribery of pity to take them. If they are a little stuffy, they certainly seem no airier because his landlady once sat upon a crimson sofa and read novels all day long. If some philanthropist builds a retreat to which she can retire gratis, and pass her declining years in regretful recollection of the crimson sofa, so let it be. Such a retreat may be dedicated to sentimental repining. But a woman of spirit and character never becomes a decayed gentlewoman, however destitute she may be.

This refusal to succumb to circumstances and to make the best of it, which is all that can be asked, is charmingly sketched in Lamb's Captain Jackson. The Captain's frugal table had the air of a feast, such was the magic of his cheerfulness. His plain cheese was served like Stilton or Roquefort, and slipping a shred of it upon his guest's plate, he contented himself with the rind, gayly declaring that the nearer the bone the sweeter the meat. Poverty was no pleasanter to him than to the rest of us. But had he gone to the almshouse he would not have complained, and in no word or sigh of his would you have discovered that he had seen better days.

The family of Captain Jackson is by no means extinct. The other day the Easy Chair met one of them in Broadway—an elderly gentleman in a well-brushed, exceedingly threadbare suit, moving briskly along the pavement. His greeting was alert and courteous. There was a little chat of the day's news, a gay jest or two, and then good-morning. Half a century ago this was a young man about town, the heir of a fortune, a youth of "family" who dressed and drove and dined and danced like the golden youth of to-day. When the first Italian opera troupe came, he was nightly behind the scenes. In the circle of Knickerbocker wits he was one. He wrote verses, and had a kind of literary name. His portrait was published in a weekly paper. He sat at the good tables. His name was Fortunio.

Everything is gone but the cheerful spirit. Nobody knows exactly how he lives, but only that it is in extreme poverty. But he preserves the tone of prosperity. He writes notes in a beautiful and graceful hand upon very cheap paper. "You remember our conversation the other morning about 'Anstey's Bath Guide'; and if you will look in your Fraser for this month, you will find that I was right." Here is the assumption that every gentleman takes Fraser, and that your correspondent may have dipped into his before you have looked at yours. Doubtless he had seen it—at some reading-room, perhaps, or on Brentano's counter.

One day we had spoken of a famous author. A little while afterwards came a comely package containing an old and choice work of his, and a note: "Dear Easy Chair,—I thought it might be a pleasure to you to own this rather uncommon copy of an author whom you evidently admire, and which it is a pleasure to my shelves to spare." What a fine air of elegant leisure in a library! But the "shelves" were a few remnant books, probably worthless to sell, but affording the friendly soul true satisfaction in giving. Fortunio is not a decayed gentleman. His gentility, in the best sense, is in full vigor. Everything but that, indeed, is decayed. But there is no unmanly moping about better days, although in few men's lives could there be a sharper contrast between the past and the present.

This cheerful steadiness is largely due to temperament, but it is not therefore beyond those who have not the same temperament. Character can emulate it. "It's bad enough to be poor," said one of the Captain Jackson family, "but it's a great deal worse to be sulky too." It is very easy, indeed, for prosperity to preach resignation to adversity, and to urge it to bear up bravely. But it is a true gospel, although it be easy to preach. Pure Lacrima Christi is as precious when poured from a glass of Murano as from a pewter mug.

THE PHARISEE

THERE is no more beautiful and impressive passage in the New Testament than that which contrasts the Pharisee thanking God that he is not as other men are and the Publican who asks mercy as a sinner. But there is no passage, also, which has been more ingeniously perverted, and it is exceedingly amusing to hear Jeremy Diddler or Robert Macaire or Dick Turpin railing at honest and industrious men as Pharisees because they prefer honesty and industry to knavery.

The taste for honesty and sobriety seems natural and simple enough, and the qualities themselves quite as valuable as those of Diddler, or even of Jonathan Wild the Great. But Jonathan will have none of them. They are Pharisaic impertinences. They are impracticable and visionary speculations, which assume heaven while yet we stand upon the green earth; and Mr. Wild, who assures us that he does not desire to pass himself off as better than other men, declares, with the noble candor which distinguishes him, that simple, downright dishonesty is good enough for him. He does not, indeed, choose that precise word, but he conveys that precise idea.

'Tis a good trick, and it is generally sure of applause. But it is only another version of a familiar maxim, that when you have no argument, you must abuse the plaintiff's attorney. As a matter of fact, your client did steal the handkerchief, or forge the name, or fire the barn. But I ask you, gentlemen of the jury—you may well say—and I appeal to all good citizens, is not this ostentation of superior virtue, this fine air of moral indignation toward my client simply because he happened to slip his hand into the wrong pocket, a little suspicious? Are we angels? I ask your honor is this work-a-day world the celestial seat and the Mount of Vision, and is a man so very much better than his fellows merely because he rolls up his sanctimonious eyes with the Pharisee and thanks God that he is holier than other men? Nay, gentlemen, have we not in this sublime and immortal parable a Divine warning against this Phariseeism which denounces the slides and slips of our common frail humanity? I ask you, gentlemen, by your verdict not to place a premium upon that most odious of all repulsive arrogancies—Phariseeism.

But it is upon the political platform that the gibes and sneers at Phariseeism are intended to be most stinging. The Honorable Jonathan Wild the Great comes out strong, as his henchmen truly declare, against his political opponents. With one vast comprehensive sneer he brands them as Pharisees, as if he were snorting consuming fire. It is not surprising, because they have had their eye upon Jonathan. They have seen him in bad company. They have caught him "conveying" public treasure. They know all about him, and he knows that they know all about him. He called himself Tweed, and he made a mesh of statutes to legalize robbery. But how good he was to the poor! How he distributed coal to the chilly! How he planted pinks and daisies in the City Hall Park, and made the Battery to bloom as the rose! How he received wedding gifts for his daughter from our best citizens; and how generously they subscribed to erect his statue to commemorate that bright flower of the State! And now a sneaking, mousing gang of would-be archangels prate about common honesty, and demand that public hands shall be clean hands! Fellow-citizens, Jonathan Wild is a man of the people. He doesn't pretend to be higher and purer and better than other men. He didn't graduate at a college, indeed, and he never read the Iliad in the original Greek. No, fellow-citizens, there is no cambric handkerchief and oh-de-cologne about him. He is just one of the boys. He whoops it up with the plain people, and, thank God, whatever he is, he is not a Pharisee.

The argument is ingenious. It does not deny that he is a thief. It only insists that those who assert it are Pharisees—and Pharisees are so odious that it is much better to scoff at them than to punish Mr. Wild. There was a good old countryman who had been early taught to take men as they are, which means to consider them liars and rascals. One day a neighbor remarked to him that he thought that the old man had lost the money with which he bought voters, because, he said, while they take your money, the other side take their votes. "The deuce they do!" said the old countryman. "Yes," said the other; "and you will find, in the long-run, that political honesty is the best political policy." "You think so, do you?" was the reply. "Well, do you know that you're a blanked metaphysical Pharisee?"

It is obvious that when the advocacy of common honesty in any relation of life is savagely and scornfully decried as Phariseeism, it is because somebody's withers are wrung. It is a plea of guilty. It is the cry of Squeers when the picture of Dotheboys Hall was displayed to the world: "I didn't do it." If a man demands honesty in politics, and it is retorted, "You're a Pharisee," it is because the dishonesty cannot be denied or disproved, and the retort is therefore a summons to all honest men to look out for thieves. To deride the demand for decency is to concede that anything but indecency is impracticable. If it be only Pharisees who insist that sugar shall not be sanded, that milk shall not be swill-fed, that coffee shall not be chiccory, that nutmegs shall not be wood, that cloth shall not be shoddy, that employés of the government shall not be forced to pay for their places, that public officers shall be honest, and that government shall not be venal, it is pleasant to think how many intelligent, upright, industrious, and practical Americans are Pharisaical.

LADY MAVOURNEEN ON HER TRAVELS

THE passenger in the crowded street railway car is often disturbed by the conscious absorption of his masculine neighbors in their newspapers when a woman enters and looks for a seat. If she be young and pretty, there are apparently seats enough, however great the crowd, and even if a man is slow to rise, he may yet, with Mr. Readywit, exhort his son sitting upon his knee to get up and give the lady his seat. The impatient passenger, in his indignation at the want of courtesy upon the part of others, sometimes forgets, indeed, to rise himself. But there is always some Nathan comfortably seated farther away whose amused look says to the impatient but stationary David, "Thou art the man."

It would be very unfair to generalize from this frequent situation that the American is uncourteous. On the contrary, he is the most truly polite man among men of all nations. Lady Mavourneen, who is familiar with the society and the manners of many countries, and who has been always accustomed to hear Americans in Europe described everywhere and with pungent emphasis as "those Americans," was amazed upon coming here to find universal courtesy. "In the street or at the railway station," she said, "if I ask anybody any question, I receive the most prompt and polite reply. Everybody is at my service, not with much bowing or flourishing, but heartily and honestly. I have never seen such universal courtesy." When she was asked whether she had observed the absorption of the street-car passengers in their newspapers, she smiled and said that she had never been obliged to stand, because some one was sure to rise. But in Paris she said that often as she was passing to a seat Monsieur Crapeaud, raising his hat politely, and saying, warmly, Pardon! pressed by and secured the seat.

Lady Mavourneen, who tells a little story with great humor, described a scene in a crowded church in Paris. An apparent lady was disturbing everybody by pushing along toward a distant chair in the row, when Lady Mavourneen arose to allow her to pass more easily, and the apparent lady immediately slipped into my lady's chair, and held it fast, saying only, in reply to her earnest remonstrance: "Madame, you left the chair; I took it. You have lost it. Voilà!" A vagabond of this kind took the seat of a gentleman who had risen to help a lady off a street car. When the gentleman returned he mentioned to the interloper that it was his seat. The interloper shrugged his shoulders, remarked that it was an empty seat when he took it, and that he should continue to occupy it. "If you don't get out of that seat, I'll take you out," was the rejoinder of the gentleman, whose shoulders were broad. The squatter scowled and abdicated.

Lady Mavourneen found, what every lady will find, that she could travel everywhere in "the States" alone, with entire safety and surrounded by the utmost courtesy. The word "lady" with which she will be accosted by hackmen and porters and conductors is spoken with kindly respect, and even if some person in a lady's garb thrusts herself into the cue of passengers slowly advancing to the window of the ticket office to buy tickets, there may be sour looks and amazed stares, but she will generally have her way. So great is our courtesy that we honor the counterfeit claim. The source of the most serious objection to the demand of suffrage for women is the secret apprehension that men will lose their sincere deference, and treat women as they treat other men, thus robbing life of the tender romance of chivalric courtesy. Emerson says of the successful lover and his mistress, "She was heaven, while he pursued her as a star; can she be heaven if she stoops to such an one as he?"

Yet, while this feeling is frequent, and seems to many very plausible, it is the true respect of the American for women which is the real strength of this very movement. The European sentiment for woman is still somewhat mediæval. She is still the goddess of the troubadours and the minnesingers, but a goddess who is treated as the South-sea Islanders treat their gods, beating them when they are not propitious. To the American she is Wordsworth's "Phantom of Delight" seen upon nearer view, and it is idle to prattle about her "sphere," as if she did not instinctively know it more truly than men. The universal courtesy which Lady Mavourneen remarked is essential respect and kindliness of feeling, which no more permits a man to gild his selfishness with a "Pardon" and a touching of his hat than it permits him to strike a woman.

Yet although courtesy is essentially in the heart, and is kind feeling rather than respectful manner, it is not worth while to despise the manner. If we must choose between the good heart and suavity of address, between Boythorne and Lovelace, of course we shall choose Boythorne. But why not both? Why not the mens sana in corpore sano? In "The Iron Pen," Longfellow says:

"And in words not idle and vain
I shall answer and thank you again
For the gift, and the grace of the gift,
O beautiful Helen of Maine!"
It is not only the gift, it is the grace in giving which completes the charm.

The young American of to-day puffs his cigarette in the face of his partner on the balcony, in the boat, or in the wagon, and smiles at the frilled Lothario of yesterday bowing in his flowered coat and paying stately compliments as stiff as her brocade to the dame whom he addresses. The youth is right in saying that the flowered coat and the stately compliment were the dress and the speech of an old sinner. But he would be right also if he remembered that familiarity breeds contempt, and that he may wisely distrust his feeling for any woman who does not put him upon his good behavior. The courtesy which Lady Mavourneen observed in the railway station and in the street was plain, but it was genuine. Respect naturally produces courtesy. Good manners are the cultivation of natural courtesy: the gift and the grace of the gift.

This was the chief remembrance, and it was a unique and precious treasure, which Lady Mavourneen carried back to Europe from America.

GENERAL SHERMAN

NONE of his great contemporaries was universally beloved more than General Sherman, perhaps none so much. The rare happiness was his not only of becoming famous by taking a great part in a great historic achievement, but of the complete enjoyment of fame. His later years forecast the future. He saw not only that his name would be remembered, but remembered with personal affection. Very few men have been able to foresee this, and very few more clearly than Sherman. It is due not to achievement alone, but to personal quality blended with achievement.

In his last years he was wholly withdrawn from public affairs, and with extraordinary tact, although constantly in the public eye and mind, and although the sense of his historic personality, so to speak, was constant, he refrained from declarations upon pending public questions, and the remarks of his interviews were not devoted to subjects of general controversy. This was doubtless the result of his accurate apprehension of his relation to the country. He had been educated by it, and had served it as a soldier. He had strong convictions and was frank of speech, but he belonged to all. He could not well be a common partisan. He was apparently untouched by political ambition. If he had felt its spur at all, he was happily able to prefer the general permanent affectionate popular regard to the fierce enthusiasm of a political campaign and the passionate ardor of partisanship.

Whatever the reason, he held aloof. Perhaps at one moment, had he assented, his name might have been caught up in a vast and tumultuous political convention, and to a burning and skilful appeal to patriotism and the still glowing memories of the war a palpitating party might have responded, and made him its leader. But if others doubted and hesitated he did not. He comprehended the situation as in a comprehensive and far-extending military movement. He knew himself, and he refused. The opportunity for which the most illustrious and the most famous of Americans have longed and labored and pined offered itself to him, unsought, unwished, and he smiled it away.

Among the chief figures of the epoch of the war probably Lincoln and Sherman were the most individual and original. The most romantic and picturesque of the many renowned events of that time was the march to the sea. It has already a distinctive character, like that of the Greeks in Xenophon's story of the ten thousand. When the news of its successful issue reached this part of the country, it served to show the simple and honest patriotism of one of the more unfortunate of the Union generals. Burnside, after the explosion of the mine at Petersburg, had been relieved, and was staying with a company of friends at a country-house on Narragansett Bay. The company were all sitting one morning upon the spacious piazza, when a messenger rode up and announced Sherman's success. Burnside's delight was enthusiastic. All thought of himself vanished. The good cause only was in his mind and heart, and, running to his wife, he joyfully kissed her, saying, "I know that the company feels as I do, and will forgive me."

It was the feeling of a soldier as simple and true-hearted and patriotic, but not so fortunate, as Sherman; and it was the same candor and manly sweetness of nature that softened Sherman's voice whenever he spoke of the soldiers of the war to whom fate had seemed to be unkind. He is gone, the last of the old familiar figures, some of his old foes bearing him tenderly to the grave. And are not Lincoln, Grant, Sherman, Sheridan, Porter, Seward, Chase, Stanton, Sumner, and their fellows, historic figures worthy to rank with the elder Revolutionary group dear to all Americans?

THE AMERICAN GIRL

A PLEASING and constant topic of English writers is the American girl. One of the later commentators says of her, "American girls have shown they can receive, travel, and live without chaperons, escorts, or husbands, and are fast developing a bright, clear, intelligent, self-reliant, courageous, and refreshing variety of the human race." And again, "Even if in future years the slender Yankee belle is hidden behind the ampler beauty of the English matron, we may still hear from her lips the wit and shrewdness, the acute accent, the intelligent question, and the rapid repartee that proclaim her original nationality." The "society" pictures in the papers and magazines represent the dismay of the British matron with marriageable daughters as she surveys the avatar of the American divinity and rival. The essential differences of society in the two countries are at once suggested, and the alarm of the watchful parent is justified.

The charm of Miss Austen's novels is their acknowledged fidelity of portraiture of the society with which they deal. They are miniatures, but the likeness is wrought with exquisite skill of detail, and as the American reader reflects he perceives that the great object of the game which they describe is eligible marriage. Indeed the motive of the novel in general is love and marriage. We open the book, we are at once introduced to Paul, and presently to Virginia, and we proceed over the pages until we hear the approaching beat of the Wedding March, which in fact we have heard from the first page, and we know that the end is at hand. But in the English novel of society, although the theme be marriage, it is not necessarily love. If that were essential, a host of rival fair ones with golden locks would bring no pang to the maternal bosom, because she would know that love will find out the one among the thousand.

The passages that we have quoted apparently describe by contrast, which is a fact which does not seem to have occurred to the writer. Doubtless at heart he is loyal to the English girl, and does not admit even in debate that her supremacy of maidenhood can be disputed. When he says that American girls have shown that they can receive, travel, and live without chaperons, escorts, or husbands, he seems to mean that they have shown this distinctively as compared with other girls. When he adds that they are fast developing a bright, clear, intelligent, self-reliant, courageous, and refreshing variety of the human race, can he mean that those words describe a new variety of girl, and that it is not perfectly familiar in England? So in the other passage, when, supposing the American girl transformed into the British matron, he remarks, with evident admiration, "we may still hear from her lips the wit and shrewdness, the acute accent, the intelligent question, and the rapid repartee that proclaim her original nationality," would he have us understand that these are not the characteristics of the British matron of to-day? Or does he intimate only that the coming of the Americans will but enlarge the number of these delightful ladies?

The writer certainly seems to describe by contrast, but he has wisely left a little cloud in which to envelop his retreat in case of emergency. Certainly we need not press him. Whatever he may think or say of the English girl, he has spoken well and truly of her American sister. His description applies to the girl who grows up amid the average conditions of American life, the girl who is portrayed in her more jejune condition in Henry James's Daisy Miller. The two chief qualities of that young woman, as represented by the shrewd and subtle artist, are self-respect and self-reliance. The perplexity of the phenomenon to the foreign reader lies in the fact that she does what the European girl without self-respect does.

A distinguished writer in New York, no longer living, once said to the Easy Chair, with an air of consternation: "Do you know that the best girls in New York go without escort to the matinées at the Academy? Goodness knows what will be the end of it!" The good man was seriously troubled. He seemed to apprehend that the young woman who could go to a matinée without an escort would probably run off with a circus troupe, and presently ride—in a very short skirt—bare-backed horses in the ring. He evidently felt that the young women whom he had seen were in grave danger of losing maidenly reserve, and that their conduct betrayed a want of refinement of feeling. The secret of his alarm lay in the fact that the social conventions of foreign society had acquired in his mind the force of rules of morality. He shared the feelings of the delightful lady who remarked that in her opinion it was immodest to go abroad without gloves. Nothing is more common than this confusion of mind, and one of the advantages of genuinely American society is that it dissipates such illusions. The Lady Mavourneen, who was familiar with the finest society both in France and

England, said that the respect shown to women in this country was so sincere and universal that she should not hesitate to cross the continent alone. Why, then, should the Easy Chair's friend have been troubled that young women went unattended to the concert at the Academy? Every man there would have been their instant defender against insult. But they went, and they were allowed to go, because the insult was more improbable than fire, while the defence was sure.

In what is called distinctively society in large cities there is a great deal of the feeling evinced by the observer at the Academy. There is abundant regard for misplaced conventions. Young women in Vienna and Paris who go unattended are generally working-women or another class, and as working-women are not respected by Lovelace and Lothario, they are exposed to insult. To avoid the chance of insult, therefore, a young woman must have an escort in a partially civilized city like Paris or Vienna. But no presumption lies against any woman in America. Her self-respect and self-reliance are unquestioned, and American women, old and young, are perpetually passing in railway trains by day and night from one part of the country to another, unsuspected and unsuspecting.

In a country where social classes are not permanent or rigidly defined, as hitherto in America they have not been, the daughter as well as the son of the house contemplates the possibility of self-support. In such a country the harem view of the sphere and occupation of woman, however modified, wholly disappears. The word "obey" gradually vanishes from the marriage service, or is smoothed away by interpretation. The ideal of woman changes, and, as we think in America, improves. All the excellent qualities which the London writer attributes to the American girl spring from this change, from social conditions which foster self-respect and self-reliance. The demand of the suffrage, the rise of the woman's college, the challenge to the great universities to lift up their gates that woman may come in, show no decline of the feminine ideal of woman, but its transformation from the fancy of a goddess or a toy into the old Scriptural conception of the helpmeet.

The British matron, as she scrutinizes what she may hold to be an invader of her realm, will not find that in any feminine quality or grace, even to the most exquisite taste in dress, or delicate charm of manner, or essential refinement of mind, Pocahontas defers to Boadicea. Where the American imitates the English or any other, as when the English girl affects the French, she must suffer from the inevitable inferiority of all imitation. When her self-reliance is boisterous, or without tact and fine perception, Daisy Miller will be as crude and distasteful as Lady Clara Vere de Vere is heartless and cruel. But Rosalind and Viola and Beatrice, and Tennyson's Eleanore and Adeline and Margaret, meet in the American a sister of the same lineage as their own, bred in an atmosphere most fortunate and fair.

ANNUS MIRABILIS

THIS year, the centenary of the opening of our national constitutional epoch, will be a Washington year. As on a saint's day there is a special service in his honor, so through all this year there will be especial remembrance of Washington, and natural self-congratulation that in him we have a glory beyond that of other nations. The last striking tribute to him is also most timely, for it is that of Mr. Bryce in his "American Commonwealth," whose publication happily coincided with the opening of this annus mirabilis. He says, in speaking of Hamilton's death, "One cannot note the disappearance of this brilliant figure, to Europeans the most interesting in the earlier history of the republic, without the remark that his countrymen seem to have never, either in his lifetime or afterward, duly recognized his splendid gifts." The explanation of this seeming want of appreciation is, however, very characteristic, for it lies in the instinctive American regard for morality.

Mr. Bryce touches it when he proceeds: "Washington, indeed, is a far more perfect character. Washington stands alone and unapproachable, like a snow-peak rising above its fellows into the clear air of morning, with a dignity, constancy, and purity which have made him the ideal type of civic virtue to succeeding generations. No greater benefit could have befallen the republic than to have such a type set from the first before the eye and mind of the people." That benefit is incalculable, and it will be acknowledged with every form of stately ceremonial and of eloquent enthusiasm during this year.

The great event of 1789 was Washington's inauguration as President, and it is the most important event in the annals of the city. The cosmopolitan character of the city from its settlement and in the early time of the little town, when it was said that more than a dozen different languages were spoken in its streets, down to the present, when it is the third or fourth city in size upon the globe, has always checked the sentiment of local pride which is so great a force in the development of a community. Among all the original States New York has seemed to care least for its significant events and its great men. That the Revolution was tactically largely a contest for the control of the Hudson, that the contest culminated at Saratoga, and that the new national order which resulted from the Revolution began in the city of New York, are facts which are known, indeed, but which have not grown into a proud tradition universally cherished and constantly repeated and celebrated like similar great events in New England.

This year, however, the last event, Washington's inauguration, will be the occasion of a great national observance. The President and cabinet, Senators and Representatives and judges, distinguished delegates from every State, will attend, and there will be religious and oratorical exercises and civil and military display. One fact, indeed, invests such a celebration with especial triumph. It is that while the government which was organized a hundred years ago was unprecedented in form and wholly untried in the experience of states, and while it was regarded with interest but with incredulity as essentially unequal to the great shocks of fate to which other states have succumbed, it has passed, within the century, not only unshaken but strengthened, through the most tremendous and prolonged ordeal to which such a government could be submitted.

Chief among its extraordinary good fortunes at its organization was that of the presence of a man without whom at that time its establishment would have been hardly possible. The French Minister at the time of the inauguration wrote home to his government that it was the universal confidence in Washington which secured assent to the Constitution. John Lamb, who was unfriendly to the Constitution, told Hamilton in Wall Street that only his faith in Washington overcame his repugnance to it. The hour had plainly come for union, but except for the man it is probable that union would not then have been effected.

The value of Washington to his country transcends that of any other man to any land. Take him from the Revolution, and all the fervor of the Sons of Liberty would seem to have been a wasted flame. Take him from the constitutional epoch, and the essential condition of union, personal confidence in a leader, would have been wanting. Franklin, when the work of the Constitutional Convention was completed, said that until then he had not been sure whether the sun depicted above the President's chair was a rising or a setting sun, but now his doubt was solved. Yet it was not the symbolic figure above the chair, it was the man within it, which should have forecast the great result to that sagacious mind.

From the moment that independence was secured no man in America saw more clearly the necessity of national union, or defined more wisely and distinctly the reasons for it. He is the chief illustration in a popular government of a great leader who was not also a great orator. Perhaps that fact gave a solid force to his influence by depriving all his expressions of a rhetorical character, and preserving in them throughout a simplicity and moderation which deepened the impression of his comprehensive sagacity. He was felt as both an inspiring and a sustaining power in the preliminary movement for union, and by natural selection he was both President of the Convention and the head of the government which it instituted. John Adams was Vice-President, and Hamilton and Jefferson were in the cabinet. After Washington himself, they were the three most eminent figures in the country. But it is not possible to conceive any one of them organizing and establishing the new system without controversy which would have rent it asunder.

Indeed this year commemorates the auspicious beginning of the most arduous task which devolved upon Washington, and which transcends that to which any other man in history has been called. Yet how little in his performance of that task his countrymen would change! During the course of the century they have been divided largely upon views of the Constitution and upon principles of administration, and have engaged in a long and momentous civil war, but they would certainly not desire that any chief act of Washington's administration should have been other than it was. He acted without precedent, but with the calm majesty of rectitude, and although the serpent of party spirit struck at him as he retired, no honest partisan to-day either distrusts his motives or doubts his wisdom.

It is a benignant fortune that so great a celebration as that of this year is an act of homage to so great a man. It was his happiness to know the affectionate reverence in which he was held. The memoirs and letters of the time show that Washington's was not a tardy and posthumous greatness, but that those who knew him best honored him most, and that America was conscious of the worth of her chief citizen. One of the most striking contemporary personal tributes to him is that of John Bernard, the English actor, who was in this country at the close of the last century, and who met Washington near the end of his life, by chance and without knowing him, near Mount Vernon.

Bernard had paid a visit to a friend upon the banks of the Potomac, and was returning upon horseback to Alexandria behind a chaise which seemed to be in difficulties, and was presently upset. The actor hastened to the rescue simultaneously with another horseman, and after some exertions they succeeded in placing the occupants of the chaise—a man and woman, who were fortunately not injured—again upon their way. After their departure Bernard's companion politely offered to dust his coat, and in returning the favor Bernard made a close survey of his companion.

"He was a tall, erect, well-made man, evidently advanced in years, but who seemed to have retained all the vigor and elasticity resulting from a life of temperance and exercise. His dress was a blue coat buttoned to his chin and buckskin breeches. Though the instant he took off his hat I could not avoid the recognition of familiar lineaments—which, indeed, I was in the habit of seeing on every sign-post and on every fire-place—still I failed to identify him."

Washington recognized Bernard as the actor whom he had "had the pleasure of seeing perform" in Philadelphia during the previous winter, and after some pleasant chat an invitation to ride with him to Mount Vernon, only a mile distant, revealed to Bernard the name of his companion. He was profoundly impressed, and upon reaching Mount Vernon they found that Mrs. Washington was indisposed, and the General ordered refreshments into a little parlor looking upon the Potomac.

At some length his guest describes the commanding presence of Washington, in which "a feeling of awe and veneration stole over you." During a conversation of an hour and a half "he touched on every topic that I brought before him with an even current of good sense, if he embellished it with little wit or verbal elegance."

"When I mentioned to him the difference I perceived between the inhabitants of New England and of the Southern States, he remarked: 'I esteem those people greatly; they are the stamina of the Union, and its greatest benefactors. They are continually spreading themselves, too, to settle and enlighten less favored quarters. Dr. Franklin is a New-Englander.' When I remarked that his observations were flattering to my country, he replied, with great good-humor: 'Yes, yes, Mr. Bernard, but I consider your country the cradle of free principles, not their arm-chair. Liberty in England is a sort of idol; people are bred up in the belief and love of it, but see little of its doings. They walk about freely, but then it is between high walls; and the error of its government was in supposing that after a portion of their subjects had crossed the sea to live upon a common, they would permit their friends at home to build up those walls about them.'

"A black coming in at this moment with a jug of spring-water, I could not repress a smile, which the General at once interpreted. 'This may seem a contradiction,' he continued, 'but I think you must perceive that it is neither a crime nor an absurdity. When we profess, as our fundamental principle, that liberty is the inalienable right of every man, we do not include madmen or idiots; liberty in their hands would become a scourge. Till the mind of the slave has been educated to perceive what are the obligations of a state of freedom, and not to confound a man's with a brute's, the gift would insure its abuse. We might as well be asked to pull down our old warehouses before trade has increased to demand enlarged new ones. Both houses and slaves were bequeathed to us by Europeans, and time alone can change them—an event, sir, which, you may believe me, no man desires more heartily than I do. Not only do I pray for it on the score of human dignity, but I can clearly foresee that nothing but the rooting out of slavery can perpetuate the existence of our Union, by consolidating it in a common bond of principle.'"

At the end of a century which has vindicated his view so nobly and so completely it is pleasant to read these words, and in this new and vivid glimpse of our Washington to find only a stronger title to our veneration. Bernard recalls the words of De Chastellux:

"The great characteristic of Washington is the perfect union which seems to subsist between his moral and physical qualities, so that the selection of one would enable you to judge of all the rest. If you are presented with medals of Trajan or Cæsar, the features will lead you to inquire the proportions of their persons; but if you should discover in a heap of ruins the leg or arm of an antique Apollo, you would not be curious about the other parts, but content yourself with the assurance that they were all conformable to those of a god."

STATUES IN CENTRAL PARK

IN 1889.

THE Easy Chair recently spoke of the statue of Longfellow which has been erected in the city of Portland, where he was born, and "Charter Oak," writing from Connecticut, asks why there is as yet no statue of Washington Irving in Central Park, the beautiful sylvan resort of his native city of New York. It is a question which the Easy Chair has already asked, and which must constantly suggest itself in the spacious public grounds which are becoming the most comprehensive of Walhallas. The London Times calls Westminster Abbey "our Walhalla," meaning that of England only. But the pleasure-ground of New York is truly a Pantheon. It is dedicated to all the gods except its own. With unwonted metropolitan modesty the city honors especially those who are not children of New York.

Webster is there, but not John Jay; Shakespeare and Scott and Burns and Dante and Halleck even, but not Irving. It is grotesque that a space set apart in New York for recreation, and decorated with marbles and bronzes commemorating illustrious men, and among them authors and statesmen, should still lack a fitting memorial of the greatest statesman and the greatest author who were born in the city. Webster's famous panegyric of Jay, that when the ermine of the Chief-Justiceship fell upon his shoulders it touched nothing that was not as pure as itself, suggests that a statue of John Jay might be of peculiar service as an object of admonitory meditation in the bowery seclusion of a city that more recently contemplated a statue to Tweed. In Couture's picture of the "Decadence of the Romans," behind the luxurious and voluptuous groups of intoxicated revellers in the foreground stand in sad severity the statues of the elder Romans surveying the scene. In the lofty aspect of Jay, filling with calm dignity the seclusion of some winding walk, would there be felt amazement and reproof? Is it to escape the sculptured rebuke of contrast with the civic heroes of to-day that it is not seen, and that the eye of the student who reflects that the city of New York has contributed few very great names to our history seeks in vain the statue of John Jay in Central Park?

Irving has every claim to this especial distinction. It is his kindly genius which made the annals of New Amsterdam the first work of our creative literature, and which invested the great river of New York with imperishable romance. Undoubtedly he wrote those annals in characters of rollicking fun, and even over the heroism of the doughty Peter Stuyvesant he has cast a humorous halo. But not all our authors combined are so identified with New York as Irving. His earlier squib of "Salmagundi" treats "the town" with an arch memory of the Spectator loitering in London, and his spell was such that in a later day Dennett, in the Nation, happily nicknamed the work of the talent which he had quickened the Knickerbocker literature.

The same genius in a tenderer mood colored the shores of the Hudson with the softest hues of legend. The banks at Tarrytown stretching backward to Sleepy Hollow, the broad water of the Tappan Zee, the airy heights of the summer Katskill, were mere landscape, pleasing scenery only, until Irving suffused them with the rosy light of story, and gave them the human association which is the crowning charm of landscape. In many a scene a hundred mountain ranges survey the lower land far reaching to the ocean. The scene is grand, but nameless, bare of tradition, and forgotten. But where

"The mountains look on Marathon,
And Marathon looks on the sea,"

the eye and the heart are enchanted with the story of Greece and its heroic human associations.

In the first century of our literature, which is ending, very few of our authors have laid this legendary spell upon American scenes as Irving did upon the Hudson. They have not much endeared the country to the popular imagination, like Burns and Scott in Scotland, where every hill and stream and bird and flower is reflected individually and fondly in tale and song. The Easy Chair once met at Niagara a young Scotchman who had come straight from his native land, and at every turn and glimpse upon Goat Island and along the banks of the river he fairly bubbled and murmured with the music of Burns and the other poets about Scottish streams and scenes, of which he was reminded at every step. So in his "Poems of Places" Longfellow reveals the charm which literature imparts to scenery—a charm which he illustrates in his "Nuremberg" and "Belfry at Bruges," and in his "Lost Youth," with its beautiful pictures of Portland, a poem which probably gives to a larger number of persons a more distinct and pleasing interest in that delightful city than anything else connected with it.

Irving is the magician who has cast this glamour upon New York, the roaring mart of trade, the humming hive of industry. He shows us in these crowded and hurried streets the leisurely forms of old Dutch burghers, their comely wives and buxom daughters, and their tranquil existence. Upon this very spot, which thus becomes a palimpsest, one life over-writing another, he awakens a romantic interest which gives it an endless fascination. He is thus a universal benefactor.

His Rip Van Winkle, indolent but kindly vagabond that he is, asserts the charm of a loitering life in the woods and fields, against all the tremendous energy and lucrative devotion to dollars, the overpowering crowd and crushing competition, of the whirring emporium. It is not necessary to defend poor Rip, or justify him as a moral exemplar. Pax, good Zeal-in-the-land Busy! But how soothing, as we mop our brows in the ardent struggle, and waste our lives in the furious accumulation of the means of living, to behold that figure stretched by the brook, or pleasing the children, or sauntering homeward at sunset! Other figures allure us, but still he holds his place. The new writers create their worlds. The new standards, another literary spirit, a fresh impulse, appear all around us. But still Rip Van Winkle lounges idly by, an unwasted figure of the imagination, the first distinct creation of our literature, the constant, unconscious satirist of our life.

The edicts of Fortune are caprices. Halleck, who sang of Marco Bozzaris, has his statue in the Park. Bryant still awaits his, and Irving, first of all, is without his memorial. The Germans have justly honored Humboldt in our Walhalla, the Scotch have commemorated Burns, the Italians have given to it Mazzini. The Puritan Pilgrim, ancestor of distinctive America, New England in bronze, is properly there. But where, asked the thoughtful child, reading the epitaphs in the graveyard, where be the bad people buried? Those whom the statues recall are all well and wisely honored in this most cosmopolitan of countries and of cities. But where, amid Germans and Italians and Scotchmen and great New-Englanders—where be the New-Yorkers?

THE GRAND TOUR

NOBODY could have written this book—a London Review recently said of Longfellow's "Hyperion"—who could have reached the Rhine in a few hours. It needed the ocean, thought the critic, to make the Rhine and Switzerland remote and romantic to the poet. But he forgot "Childe Harold," a book written by an Englishman, which has given to the Rhine and Italy a more romantic glamour for John Bull upon his travels than any book he reads. It is not the distance, it is the imagination susceptible to association which is the secret.

The traveller of to-day is not likely to be affected as his father was by the melancholy melody of Byron; but it is an interesting illustration of the power of his genius that Byron has imposed his interpretation of so many scenes upon the mind of the modern English and American observer. His view makes Italy, as Sir Thomas Lawrence's portrait of John Kemble made Hamlet. If we stand in the Capitol and look at the Dying Gladiator, we must also see "his young barbarians all at play" upon the Danube. If at Terni we see the Velino "cleave the wave-worn precipice," the Byronic lines murmur along our lips. As we step into the gondola and glide gently upon the Grand Canal, memory keeps time to the measure of the dipping oar with the words whose charm is unexhausted:

"In Venice Tasso's echoes are no more,
And silent rows the songless gondolier."

At "a tomb in Arqua," at "Clarens, sweet Clarens," we are still led, like Dante, by the singing guide. The Guide-book is full of him. The travel-books are full of him. He is familiar almost to commonplace. Who comes to "Belgium's capital" for the first time without listening for "the sound of revelry"? Who goes to the field of Waterloo remembering "the unreturning brave," and does not sigh,

"And Ardennes waves above them her green leaves."

Sitting quietly here in a great land which looks to the future, not to the past, it is pleasant to think of the throngs of travellers who have gone hence for a summer wandering in Europe. Yet so intense is the delight of European travel, so freshly remembered is it when almost another generation of travellers are ready to begin their journey, that the patriarch who goes to the wharf to say farewell to the newer voyagers looks at them with tenderness and pity, and there is even a sadness in his congratulations, not because they are sailing away, but because he cannot believe that they will find what he found, nor possibly enjoy what he enjoyed. These newer voyagers will see a France and a Switzerland and an Italy; they will eat oranges at Sorrento, and gaze upon the Mediterranean from Capri, and hear the fisher's song at Amalfi: but they will not hear and see through the enchantment of lapsed years.

In his lively book of travelling letters Dr. Bellows says that he went up the Nile in a steamer of seventy berths. An ancient mariner of the Nile cannot comprehend it. In a steamer? With paddles or screws whisking the water? And steam blowing off? Making innumerable miles a day? The round trip to Philæ in two weeks, or a week? But how could you see Egypt, or feel it? That slow floating southward upon white wings; the sinking deeper and farther from the world we knew; the sense of infinite strangeness and distance; the weeks passing with no sign of accustomed life; slowly, one by one, the temples, the tombs; in the still days the crew dragging the boat along and singing the wild minor refrain; a voyage of wonder and of dreams—is that Egypt to be seen in a steamer? It is useless to say that you may go in the old way if you choose. You cannot go in the old way, because it is no longer what it was, if there be a newer. You may drive from London to Oxford. But is that going by the old English stage-coach when it was the only way, when the guard wound his horn, and the cherry-nosed coachman threw down the ribbons at each relay, and the neat inns stood smiling with open doors, and tra-la-la sped the nimble team by the park gate and the hawthorn hedge? You may go by sloop from New York to Albany. But is that now the romantic Hudson voyage which it was when it could be made in no other way?

No sensible ancient mariner will quarrel with all this, nor desire to banish the steamer of seventy berths from the Nile. When he shakes a farewell hand with the youth who are going to run up to Rome by train, and are not going to stop at a certain point upon the Campagna, and run forward to the top of a hill whence they can see far away upon the horizon the faintly outlined dome of St. Peter's—and who are not going from Leghorn to Florence through the grape harvest, their carriage heaped with the luscious clusters, but are to whiz through Tuscany in an hour or so, the regret in his tone is not personal or selfish, it is for a whole order of things passed away.

Such an ancient mariner would, however, be indeed sorry if he supposed that anybody suspected him of a very common and very odious kind of remark, against which he kindly warns all the throngs of travellers of whom mention has been made. The remark in question may be called the capping remark. Thus one traveller says to another—as Marco Polo to George Sandys—

"You went to Jerusalem?"

"Yes."

"And to Jericho?"

"Yes."

"And to the Jordan?"

"Yes."

"Did you see the white stone on the bottom near where the river flows into the Dead Sea?"

"Well—let me see! I don't exactly seem to remember that I did precisely see that."

"Ah!" replies Marco Polo.

It is a very brief sound, but being interpreted it means, "Then, my dear George Sandys, you might just as well not have seen the Jordan at all." Not that the white stone was famous or worth seeing, but that Marco Polo wished to "rub in" upon George Sandys's mind the conviction that he, Polo, had seen more than he, Sandys, in the same direction.

This capping process sometimes leads to very droll results. Young Green heard Gray and Brown comparing their notes of travel. Each was naturally anxious to have seen and done rather more than the other; but it appeared that each had been in about the same places, and had had very much the same experience.

"Lago Maggiore is a lovely sheet of water," remarked Gray.

"Truly exquisite," replied Brown.

"And Isola Bella is most beautiful," suggested Gray.

"Dear me! dear me!" approvingly assented Brown.

"How high is the statue of San Carlo Borromeo?" asked Gray.

"About sixty feet," answered Brown.

"It's a wonderful prospect from his eye," said Gray.

"Whose eye?" asked Brown.

"San Carlo Borromeo's," replied Gray, whose mind instantly suspected that he had caught the adversary, and who followed up his advantage vigorously and suddenly. "Of course you went up San Carlo?"

"Up San Carlo? You mean the church at—"

"Oh no! the statue on Lago Maggiore."

"Went up the statue! what do you mean?" snapped Brown, foreseeing discomfiture.

"Oh! I thought you probably knew," retorted the triumphant Gray, "that the statue is hollow."

"Oh! ah! yes!" returned Brown, indifferently.

"And you didn't go up?" pressed Gray.

"Not exactly," feebly rejoined Brown.

"Nor sit in his nose?" continued Gray.

"Not exactly," muttered Brown.

"Nor look out of his eyes?" said Gray.

"I thought I wouldn't," murmured Brown, in full retreat.

"Oh!" smiled Gray, with the air of David holding the head of Goliath by the hair, and displaying it to mankind—"oh!"

Young Green heard all this, and he resolved that whatever he did not do when he went to Europe, he would at all hazards sit in the nose of San Carlo Borromeo. The next year he came to Lago Maggiore. He saw the statue. He remembered the conversation and his high resolve, and he essayed the deed. It was fearful. He tore his hands; he tore his clothes; he was half suffocated; and, wedging himself into the nose, he stuck fast, and was only rescued at the peril of his life. When he told Gray afterward, and reminded him of the colloquy with Brown, that experienced traveller laughed until the tears ran down his cheeks. "My dear Green," said he, "I never went up the confounded thing; but it was necessary to take Brown down somehow, and I employed the good saint for the purpose." He laughed again to tears; but Mr. Green soberly resolved that he would eschew the capping talk of travel. And he chose the wiser course.

The truth is that Green should not trust too much the tales, nor indeed the regrets, of the ancient mariners.

"For travellers tell no idle tales,
But fools at home believe them."

Certainly when this one remarks that he feels in saying farewell that young Green will never see the Europe that he saw, he has not the remotest idea of dimming his bright hope nor of asserting an advantage. What is it, indeed, but a way of saying that he is no longer the same man he was? If he were, what would be the gain of travel? It is not only an enlargement of the scenery of the mind, not only a richer and more various memory that he has acquired, but a riper experience. He has grown wiser; and perhaps all that he feels when he shakes Green's parting hand is that Green is not so wise as he will one day be.

EASY DOES IT GUVNER

DICKENS'S Rogue Riderhood, who says "Easy does it, guvner," was a very practical man. But there is no motto which is more susceptible of perversion. Mr. Seward said the same thing in his last great speech. "I early learned from Jefferson that in politics we must do what we can, not what we would." It is not only plausible, but it is true. Yet its truth can be most readily abused to defeat everything for which it is urged.

"'I weep for you,' the walrus said;
'I deeply sympathize.'
With tears and sobs he sorted out
Those of the largest size,
Holding his pocket-handkerchief
Before his streaming eyes."

It was necessary that the walrus should eat, and it was very sad that the oysters should satisfy the necessity. But it is obvious that wicked walruses who have no intention whatever of not eating oysters would sob aloud with heart-rending vehemence as proof of a virtue which they do not possess. The foes of progress are always anxious that its friends should go easily. "Easy does it, guvner." But meanwhile they are anything but easy in obstructing. In the race, the sly gentleman who bets on Tom whispers confidentially to the jockey who rides Jerry that he had better "go easy." The friends of the saloon hope that the true friends of temperance are aware that the only way of success is to avoid fanaticism. But they omit to hide their bodies as well as their heads, for they are unsparing fanatics on their own behalf.

When Gustavus, in deference to his dear Griselda, promised to begin to reform the baleful habit of smoking, his Griselda was jocund as the dawn. But at the end of a week she did not observe that there were fewer cigars consumed, and she pleasantly asked him if the good resolution had escaped his memory. "By no means," he answered; "quite the contrary. But you remember what Rogue Riderhood said, 'Easy does it, guvner.' We must move warily upon the intrenched enemy, dearest Grizzle. Remember that Rome was not built in a day." Griselda remembered faithfully. But still the cigars continued, and upon a further gentle remonstrance Gustavus rejoined: "Certainly; but we must be reasonable. There are many steps, my dear Griselda. In siege operations the great masters of war approach by parallels, after making ample and thorough preparation. That is what I am doing. I am beginning to prepare to begin. Easy does it, you know. Don't forget Rome."

Still Gustavus smoked, and still Griselda waited, and at the end of six months she asked with a smile how far he had advanced in abandoning the habit of smoking. "Dear Grizzle," he answered, "you remember the weeds that sprang up and soon withered because they had no depth of soil. I wish my reform of this naughty habit to be well rooted, that it may long endure. None of your spasmodic virtue, your superficial goodness, for me! Great reforms, even in personal habits, my dear Mrs. Gustavus, cannot be accomplished in a day. Even Rome was not built in that time. I am working for great results, to which all my tastes and habits must conform. I must lay the foundations broad and deep. Easy does it, my rose-bud."

Gustavus continues to smoke, and Easy continues to do it. But there is another saying quite as wise as that of Rogue Riderhood, which exhorts him who puts his hand to the plough not to look back. The trouble with Riderhood's apothegm is that it supplies an endless excuse for not doing it. If the habit is too strong, and will not budge, you can soothe your conscience and make the most plausible of pleas by insisting that human nature and long custom and uniform tradition and the honest doubt whether smoking is, after all, injurious, must all be carefully considered. That is what Dickens also calls the great art of how not to do it. "My son, if you wish a thing done, do it yourself; if not, send," said the wise father; and the pioneers, the men without whose one idea and uncompromising energy and conciliation nothing would be accomplished, say with Sumner. "There is but one side," and with Cato, "Delenda est Carthago."

It is true that everything cannot be done at once, but something must be done all the time; and you will observe that it is not when the work is advancing, but when it stops or goes backward, that we hear the familiar wisdom of the Rogue that Easy does it. That is what makes it a suspicious saying, "What are you doing, sir?" thundered the master to the boy. "Nothing, sir," replied the frightened pupil. "Just as I thought, sir. Don't you know that your business is to do something?" When a man says "Easy does it," he may be doing all that he can but the immense probability, the almost absolute certainty, is that he is doing nothing, or, like the amiable

Gustavus, he is "beginning to prepare to begin."

SISTE VIATOR

IT is still very difficult to discover where the bad people are buried. The cemeteries are still symbolically white with monuments to the departed. Shylock and Ralph Nickleby are still, upon their tombstones, the most respected of deceased citizens. Here lies Clytemnestra, a model of the wifely virtues, whom an inconsolable spouse deplores. Beneath this marble, in the tranquil hope of a joyful resurrection, repose the remains of Iago, who kept the noiseless tenor of his way. Beyond sleeps Solomon, most faithful of husbands; and under this turf of buttercups and daisies lie Paris and Lovelace, arcades ambo, too early lost. 'Tis pathetic to reflect how much worthier is the world under-ground than that which still cumbers its surface; and if we, whose lives are indifferent honest, had only had the good fortune to die a century ago, our memories would by this time have been upon our tombstones a very odor of sanctity to the sense of the age which knows us, perhaps, but too well.

In one of his terrible inscriptions suggested for the monuments of the Georges, Thackeray says, "He left an example for youth and for age to avoid. He never did well by man or by woman." Has there been only one such George in the world? And if more, and in every age, in what cemetery have you found their epitaphs? Catiline was a fascinating and accomplished man. He had many followers, and if his political views and projects were open to differences of opinion, he was certainly well-mannered. Has there been but one Catiline in history? Or is he confined wholly to a public sphere? Cicero described him as "a corrupter of youth," and no one has denied it. Where is Catiline buried? If you sought his grave by that epitaph, where would you find it? Is there no corrupter of youth now? Have there been none within the last century? None, if you may trust the epitaphs. How long will you abuse our patience, O Catiline, and be annually buried,

113

like Cato the Censor, with crosses of white camellias laid upon your coffin, and wreaths of immortelles hung upon the weeping effigy of Virtue which guards your sleep?

But because a man was brutal and coarse and cruel in his life, must we needs insist upon it when he is gone? When Mawworm leaves us, must we write upon his grave, he lying below defenceless, "Hic jacet a hypocrite"? When old Sathanas departs to a sphere of light and truth, shall we carve upon his monument, "Father of lies"? Is it manly? Shall we have no mercy? Do we really know any man; and shall charity be forgotten? To be human is to be frail; and is not the fact that we must die at all, of which the grave is proof, itself sufficient comment upon our weakness? Here lies Colonel Newcome—tender, generous, noble, child-like heart! Shall we add that he was credulous and ignorant? Dear Uncle Toby is in the next grave. Shall we shout in marble, "Siste, viator, contemplate his foibles"? Sacred to the memory of Samuel Pickwick. Is the inscription incomplete if we do not chisel beneath it, "A wind-bag pricked by Death"?

Epitaphs are written more forcibly than upon tombstones. When old Silenus dies, and the white camellias and the lilies-of-the-valley and the rose-buds are strewn upon his bier, and the "universally lamented" is cut upon the monument, the satire is pathetic, but it is slight. But when the bloated old debauchee is cautiously and forgivingly praised in the papers, and everybody solemnly pretends not to know what everybody knows that everybody else does know, it is a sign not of charity, but of public demoralization. Catiline corrupts youth by his example. Then his own offences bring him to a sudden end, and the newspapers speak of him so deprecatingly, so gingerly, that as a good man being dead yet speaketh, so a bad man being dead yet corrupteth. His evil influence is not suffered to perish with him, but it is cherished and extended and confirmed, and his death, like his life, demoralizes.

Dick Turpin no longer rides in jack-boots upon Hounslow Heath, stopping my Lord Bishop and the Right Honorable the Earl of Garter; and no longer stands at the dock, the hero of St. Giles's; and goes no longer to the gallows in a blaze of glory, with a huge nosegay in his button-hole. Richard Turpin is a very different fellow in his costume of to-day, but he is the same Dick of the jack-boots and the heath, this vulgar robber who smirks and is called smart. He drives a fine equipage, and lives luxuriously, and keeps a harem, and frequents Wall Street, and beats everybody in the game of making money, and spending it profusely and splendidly. He dazzles the eyes of the widow's son, and bewilders his mind. The boy sees the money with which Richard surrounds himself by means which honorable men despise. He hears him called good-humoredly a great rascal, and sees that he buys judges, and steals vast properties, and procures laws to protect him. The boy hears that all men are fallible, and that some men are no worse than other men, and that money is a fine thing, and honor and truth and respect and all the rest of it are very well, but see what power, what pleasure, what luxury Turpin commands! Then the poor boy rushes for the same prizes, and fails, and ends in disgrace, the jail, suicide. And Dick Turpin tosses a hundred dollars to the boy's mother, and a generous press exclaims, "Not a model man, perhaps; but what noble generosity! The friend of the widow and the orphan! When he dies, how many poor homes will be darkened with grief!" Yes, and the hundred dollars probably pays the widow for her boy.

It is not difficult to be generous with the money of others. A year ago it was announced that Greed had given forty or fifty thousand dollars to the poor. "There," said the admirers of Turpin, "you may say what you will of Greed. He, too, is not a polished man; he is not a scholar nor a dainty gentleman; but he is one of the people; he is large-hearted and generous. Who else has given fifty thousand dollars to the poor?" Yes, and who else has stolen five millions? The politest gentlemen of the highway were notoriously gallant. The Marquis of Goutytoe they compelled to descend from his carriage, and sent the trudging market-woman home in it. They eased the pockets of the Spanish ambassador, and threw a doubloon to the leper hiding behind the hedge. It was a cheap munificence. So was Greed's. It was not his fifty thousand dollars, the giving of which caused such a burst of good feeling, and the exclamation, "There now!" It was only a little of the millions that were not his. He gave it to the poor dwellers in tenement-houses, and it was said that there was no wretched hovel to which he did not send a load of coal or a barrel of flour during the winter months. But he took them first from those wretched dens. Somebody paid the taxes that he stole, and it is the poor who at last pay taxes. Where be the bad people buried? When Turpin dies, we have Greed's opinion of him and his ways gravely paraded in a newspaper. Madame Brinvilliers's opinion of Lucrezia Borgia would be edifying reading!

Shall we have no charity, then? and when a man lies dead and defenceless, shall not warfare cease? Warfare may cease; but should death condone all offences? The malignant lover who denounced his rival to the Inquisition, and in the very moment of his rival's death by fire himself fell dead—shall we write over him, De mortuis? Shall we Romans, whose sons he corrupted, go dumb and sorrowing behind the corpse of Catiline? When a bad man dies, let us say that he was bad. Although he was very rich and very splendid, shall we remember only that he gave in charity one quarter of one per cent. upon the amount of his thefts? The Italian brigand chief, when his band had slaughtered the travellers, said, "There are twelve of us, and we will share equally; but the first equal share shall be for the mother of God." When we tell his story, shall we see only that share?

GEORGE WILLIAM CURTIS

CHRISTENDOM VS. CHRISTIANITY

IT is remarkable that what is called the practical sense of Christendom virtually rejects the Christian ideals as impracticable. Its highest ideal is obedience to the Divine will, and its instinct, therefore, should represent the religious man as the perfection of vigorous manhood. The more manly, the finer the bloom of health, the sounder the body for the sound and purified mind, the truer and more satisfactory the type, the more symmetrically revealed the Christian man. This is the simple and natural ideal among living men of unthwarted and normal Christian excellence.

But so little is this the fact that the oldest traditions of Christian art depict the founder of Christianity Himself not as a blooming man, not as a figure of the inward and outward health that proceeds inevitably from complete and absolute conformity to the Divine will, but as a wan and wasted personality plainly worsted by the world. This conception extends to the constant and organized control of the Church, and the general feeling of Christendom regards the ministers of its religion either as official personages or as excluded from actual knowledge of life; not masters of the arena, but professionally unfit to cope with the world.

It may, indeed, be said that the traditions of Christian art show a misapprehension of the essential character of the Christian faith. But however that may be, it is certainly true that these traditions do not misrepresent the general conception of Christianity which is professed by those who practically reject its ideals. Here goes Solomon Gunnybags to Christian worship on Sunday morning. He "abashiates" himself in his pew, and his confession that he is a miserable sinner is so sonorous and impressive that the hearer sighs sympathetically with Solomon's consciousness of the enormous burden of wrong-doing that he carries.

Now what is Solomon doing in his pew? He is solemnly professing confidence in and reverence for certain principles of faith and conduct, not only as lofty in themselves, but as absolutely essential to his soul's salvation. Then, unless the whole universe is a farce, and religion and the soul impostures, they are the most practical and practicable of all possible principles, because otherwise the soul's salvation could not be made by beneficent Omnipotence dependent upon fidelity to them. But if some attendant spirit should say to Solomon Gunnybags, as he walks home with the happy consciousness of duty done, "Solomon, the golden rule and the Christian religion forbid you to 'unload' upon David the stock that you believe to be very shaky," he would unquestionably feel, if he did not say: "Stuff! Every man for himself. Of course Christianity is an excellent thing, but it doesn't mean that." Gunnybags does not expressly repudiate Christian principle as unpractical; he only believes it to be so.

The fundamental doctrine of the Christian life is love. The Christian millennium is peace. But it is Christendom that maintains the vast standing armies; and when the International Peace Congress meets in London and proposes disarmament, the good-natured reply of Christendom is, "Well—yes—perhaps—some time," with a smile of amused incredulity, as when a child seriously asks for the moon. Yet this is Christendom, and the Christian principles are entirely familiar, and every Sunday and saint's day in all the Christian churches we protest that the practice of them is essential to our soul's salvation. Then we wipe our eyes, and smile kindly upon any one who really insists that we should offer the other cheek, and forgive seventy times seven. Oh no, we say; that is an eccentric view. No man in this world—that is, in Christendom—can afford to allow himself to be imposed upon. If we don't look out for number one, who will take charge of that precious numeral?

So it is that on some bright July day, looking in imagination upon the respectable Universal Peace Congress in the Hôtel Métropole in London, and hearing the Bishop of Durham offer a resolution for international arbitration, and denouncing the folly, the waste, the woe and wickedness and wrong of war, we hear also, not the immediate and instinctive assent of Christendom, but its wistful prayer and half-despairing hope that some time Christianity may be found to be practicable, and something more than a pretty dream. Yet is there anything more certain than that the Christendom which actually rejects the Christian ideals and principles as impracticable, denounces most savagely those who practically illustrate them, even if they theoretically reject them?

The moral of this little sermon is altogether Christian, for it is charity. Since Christendom is in practice so universally unchristian, and holds its own fundamental principles in such practical contempt, every member of that vast fraternity should be very modest in judging others. Could there be a more radically unchristian figure in human history than Torquemada? If

Christianity be what it declares itself to be, the least throb of sound Christian feeling in his bosom would have held his hand. The Inquisition, the fierceness of sects, the religious wars, offensive wars of any kind, are possible only among Christians who hold Christianity to be impracticable.

Yet when the Easy Chair saw a gentle lady going to morning prayers on a happy saint's day, and heard through the open window the murmuring music of the promise when two or three are gathered together, and marked during all the day and in daily conduct the unselfishness, the sympathy, the courtesy, the kindly care of old and young, the faithful doing of duty, the nameless charm of lofty character, the Christian ideal was no longer the mirage of an unreached and unattainable oasis in the desert; it was already come down to earth; it was here, a little heaven below.

FRANCIS GEORGE SHAW

1882.

IN beginning his tender and charming paper upon Washington Irving and Macaulay, Thackeray recalls the beautiful story of which he was so fond, of Sir Walter Scott's last words to his son-in-law Lockhart: "Be a good man, my dear; be a good man." It was a soft autumnal day. The windows were wide open. The low sound of the rippling Tweed stole into the chamber. The most renowned and the most widely beloved of living men lay dying, after a career of admiration and adulation, and of gratified ambition almost unexampled, and in the clear and serene light of the moment that shows things as they are, the one lesson and moral garnered by that marvellous life is spoken in the simple words, "Be a good man, my dear." ...

There are men whose simplicity and dignity and strength and purity of character, whose sound judgment and supreme common-sense, dispose of sophistry and artifice in all relations and pursuits, as surely and completely as the sun dries the dew. They are gentlemen, because they know other men only as men, touching electrically whatever of manhood there may be in them, and whose contact is a silent and consuming rebuke of pretence and falsehood. Whatever his own advantage or attraction or position or grace, the man of this quality takes hold of the reality in other men, man meeting man, as when the grave William of Orange, in his plain serge coat, met the brilliant Philip Sidney in his gold-flowered doublet, and neither was troubled by the clothes of the other.

Such a man lately died. The mingled strength and simplicity and sweetness of his nature, the lofty sense of justice, the tranquil and complete devotion to duty, the large and humane sympathy, not lost in vague philanthropic feeling, but mindful of every detail of relief—the sound and steady judgment, the noble independence of thought and perfect courage of conviction, the blended manliness and modesty of a life which was unstained, and of a character which seemed without a flaw, all belonged to what we call the ideal man.

Passing from college to the counting-room of a great commercial business, his sagacity, energy, and executive power were all brought into successful action. He went to Europe and to the West Indies, but much of the spirit of trade and many of its practices were uncongenial to him, and he quietly withdrew, despite wonder and affectionate remonstrance, to lead his own life in his own way. By taste and temperament an out-door man, he made his home in the rural neighborhood of Boston, busy with country cares and various studies, but interested chiefly in helping other men. He was allied by sympathy more than by much previous actual association with the founders of Brook Farm. But when they chose the site for their enterprise not far from his house, he was soon in the pleasantest relations with the leaders, for their spirit and purpose were in harmony with his own. He was a parishioner and warm personal friend of Theodore Parker, who lived near him, and his keen common-sense and mastery of practical affairs were most useful to Parker as to Ripley. Indeed, the hospitality of such a man for every generous endeavor and for all new and humane ideas was a happy augury for the philanthropic pioneers, because it seemed to promise the final approval and adhesion to their cause of the most conservative and substantial sentiment of the community.

Such a man was, of course, an abolitionist in the days when the name was as repugnant to what is called "society" as the name Christian was to the Jewish Sanhedrim or Methodist to the English Establishment a century and a half ago. He generously aided the cause, which seemed to him that of practical Christianity and of American patriotism, and he held most friendly relations with its chief representatives, who were ostracized and denounced. But his sympathy was not an abstract regard for man rather than for men, and his interest in the effort to help a race and to forecast a happier social organization did not dull his heart or close his hand to the necessities of his neighbor. His life, indeed, was a prolonged charity, but a charity directed by a singularly calm and shrewd judgment. His exhaustless generosity was not the sport of wayward impulse. It was not a well-meaning weakness, but a wise force which helped others to help themselves, but knew also when such self-help was impossible.

Yet the strength and reserve and independence of his character were such that the man was never lost in the reformer. His fine nature instinctively asserted his own individuality. He quietly shunned the wearisome artificiality of society, but he did not merge his own home in the general home of his friends and neighbors at Brook Farm, and his house was always a glimpse of the social refinement and grace, the mental and moral charm, to which the dreams of social regeneration and the elaborate fancies of Fourier pointed—fancies which greatly interested him as hints of a happier social order.

Long absence with his family in Europe, and a long and final residence upon Staten Island, only matured and developed the man, in whom not only was there no guile, but in whom even the most intimate eye could not note a fault. Clarendon might have studied from him his portrait of Falkland: "his inimitable sweetness of, and delight in, conversation; his flowing and obliging humanity; his goodness to mankind; and his primitive simplicity and integrity of life." Disinclined to public life of every kind, he was yet full of the highest public spirit, and it was but natural that his only son should have been selected by Governor Andrew to command the first colored regiment that marched from Massachusetts in the war. In his young person all that was best in the New England youth of his time, all the strength of the elder colonial and Revolutionary day, blended with all the grace and tenderness and gentleness of its modern life, the stern old Puritan softened into a humaner Bayard, was typified. It was the flower of Essex that two hundred years ago was withered in the fatal Indian ambush in the Deerfield Meadows. It was the flower of New England that fell upon a hundred redder fields within a score of years.

But no sorrow could fatally chill a faith which was reflected in the perpetual summer of the father's presence and temperament. The frank urbanity of his greeting, the hearty grasp of his hand, the lofty simplicity of his courtesy, were but the signs of that unwasting freshness of sympathy which held him true to the ideals and aims of earlier life. His helping hand reached invisibly into a hundred homes, and upheld a hundred faltering lives. But, besides this, as president of the Freedman's Aid Association his administrative skill and his wise benevolence enabled him to bear a most effective part in the great settlement of the war. His invincible modesty and scorn of ostentation veiled his beneficent activities, public and private. But nothing could veil the pure and steadfast and unwearying devotion to the well-being of other men. Kindly but firmly he protected his own seclusion, and he permitted no man, in Emerson's phrase, to devastate his day. The freshness of feeling which keeps the heart young was unwasted to the end. His full life brimming purely to the sea reflected heaven as clearly when at last it mingled with the main as when it ran a limpid rivulet from its spring. Young and old, man and boy, he was still the simplest, noblest, most devoted, best. How truly he was the man that every thoughtful man secretly wishes he might be, those only know who knew Francis George Shaw.

THE END

www.ingramcontent.com/pod-product-compliance
Lightning Source LLC
Chambersburg PA
CBHW070708290526
45790CB00001B/498